"A clear, easy-to-read guide on 'how families work'—for anyone who wants to understand themselves better."

Stan Tatkin, PsyD, MFT
couple therapist, founder of the PACT Institute,
and author of *Wired for Love*

"A fascinating, warm-hearted guide to understanding how our families shape our personalities, relationships, and emotions. Elaine Gibson's book teaches us how to explore the most important dynamics in our lives, giving us powerful insights into our own everyday patterns and habits. *Your Family Revealed* is an invaluable resource that offers readers the gift of self-awareness—as well as a few hundred 'aha' moments."

Jackson MacKenzie
author of *Whole Again* and *Psychopath Free*

"It is rare to find a self-help book that takes difficult psychological concepts and puts them in a form that is helpful to everyone's daily living. By providing workbook exercises, this book is an excellent resource for anyone who is doing their own therapeutic work, anyone who wants to know more about how to understand their family dynamics, and clinicians who want a succinct review of fundamental psychological theories. It offers helpful hints on how to handle family emotional triangles, family secrets, and dysfunctional family patterns while using wonderful real-life case examples. It is a 'must read'!"

Michael L. Chafin, MDiv, MEd, LMFT
former president of the American Association
for Marriage and Family Therapy

"It was my honor to read Elaine Carney Gibson's *Your Family Revealed*. Gibson's knowledge of family systems theory, years of clinical experience and wisdom, and generous sharing of personal stories and insight are woven together with her warm and gently guiding voice. *Your Family Revealed* uniquely combines clinical theory in an accessible format with opportunities to apply and explore the reader's own family experiences. This work is a gift to the counseling professional and beyond to anyone wishing to grow through insight about the family."

Erika Pluhar, PhD, EdS, LMFT, LPC, CST-S

"This book is packed with key issues, explained from both personal and professional perspectives, related to understanding one's family system. Garnering wisdom distilled from her 50 years of clinical work and over 35 years of training family therapists, Elaine Carney Gibson has written an engaging, intelligent, accessible book for both the lay and professional reader. It is an important book for our time, and I highly recommend it."

Catherine McCall
author of the international bestselling memoir
Never Tell, retired family therapist, and contributing
writer for *Psychology Today* magazine

"In her book, *Your Family Revealed*, Elaine Carney Gibson has managed to synthesize numerous concepts from the history of marriage and family therapy into a highly readable and applicable volume. Each thematic chapter offers theoretical perspectives gleaned from years of experience that is supported by intriguing and often entertaining examples. This is a truly helpful book for anyone who could benefit from a more enlightened understanding of the systems that we grow up in and those we create. It provides meaningful insights into the dynamics of human relationship and helps reveal the motivations and origins guiding many familial and relational challenges. Whether the reader is a therapist, an educator, or simply someone who wants a better understanding of the intricate relationship between ourselves and the systems we inhabit (as well as those that inhabit us), this accessible and informative book has much to offer."

Stuart D. Smith, LPC

"As a recently retired family law attorney, I regret that I did not have access to the caring insights into couples and families presented so beautifully by Elaine Gibson. The relationships she describes in *Your Family Revealed* clearly illuminate familial struggles, helping to give direction to solutions for ways forward, even in conflict, whether in divorce or child custody cases. This superb book should definitely be in the library of every domestic relations attorney."

Carol B. Powell
attorney-at-law, Atlanta, Georgia

"I've finally found the book that I would wish for every person exploring their path of self-discovery. Elaine Gibson's book, *Your Family Revealed*, provides us with nuggets of wisdom that help us understand ourselves and our families. If one book can widen your mind, deepen your heart, and inspire your spirit, this is it!"

Rev. Cameron Trimble

CEO of Convergence, author of *Searching for the Sacred*

"Elaine has created an illuminating work that is truly a reflection of her five decades as a psychotherapist and educator. At a time when people's curiosity about their ancestors is growing, this book can help individuals, couples, and families decipher their relationships with greater clarity and understanding. This book explains powerful concepts usually reserved for textbooks in 'user friendly' language that results in an inspired guide for one's own life."

Janet Mainor, MS, LPC, NBCC, CPCS

executive director of The Link Counseling Center

Your
FAMILY
Revealed

Your
FAMILY
Revealed

A Guide to Decoding
the Patterns, Stories, and Belief Systems
in Your Family

ELAINE CARNEY GIBSON,
LMFT, LPC

BOULDER, COLORADO

Sounds True
Boulder, CO 80306

This book is not intended as a substitute for the medical recommendations of physicians, mental health professionals, or other health-care providers. Rather, it is intended to offer information to help the reader cooperate with physicians, mental health professionals, and health-care providers in a mutual quest for optimum well-being. We advise readers to carefully review and understand the ideas presented and to seek the advice of a qualified professional before attempting to use them.

All names used throughout the book have been changed to protect patients' privacy. In all case studies, circumstances have been changed or are a composite rendering.

Published 2022

Cover design by Jennifer Miles
Book design by Meredith Jarrett

Naomi Replansky, excerpt from "An Inheritance" from *Collected Poems*. Copyright © 2012 by Naomi Replansky. Reprinted with the permission of The Permissions Company, LLC, on behalf of Black Sparrow / David R. Godine, Publisher, Inc., godine.com.

S. H. Payer, "Live Each Day to the Fullest." Reproduced by permission of American Greetings Corporation, @AGC, LLC.

Printed in the United States of America

BK06540

Library of Congress Cataloging-in-Publication Data

Names: Gibson, Elaine Carney, author.
Title: Your family revealed : a guide to decoding the patterns, stories,
    and belief systems in your family / Elaine Carney Gibson, LMFT, LPC.
Description: Boulder, CO : Sounds True, 2022. | Includes bibliographical
    references and index.
Identifiers: LCCN 2022005508 (print) | LCCN 2022005509 (ebook) | ISBN
    9781649630049 (paperback) | ISBN 9781649630056 (ebook)
Subjects: LCSH: Families--Psychological aspects. | Self-realization.
Classification: LCC HQ519 .G53 2022 (print) | LCC HQ519
    (ebook) | DDC 646.7/8--dc23/eng/20220608
LC record available at https://lccn.loc.gov/2022005508
LC ebook record available at https://lccn.loc.gov/2022005509

10 9 8 7 6 5 4 3 2 1

To my ancestors, especially my Mother and Father
and
Bobba and Grandpappy
and
Aunt Helen and Uncle Tom

My siblings and my cousins
My three sons
and
My grandchildren, who inspire me daily—
Chessel, Spencer, Stella, and Hyde

You are ALL always with me in my Heart and in my Soul.

Contents

Introduction

Our families can be a source of our greatest joys and our deepest struggles. This book is intended to help you decode your family so that you can understand your family dynamics by better understanding how family systems operate, which will allow you to more fully know yourself and anyone with whom you have relationships.

Family constellations have changed significantly in the twenty-first century. Our society began to accept and acknowledge multiracial and multicultural families, as well as single-parent families, blended families, and families with same-sex partners more fully. In addition, in past generations families tended to live in proximity, whereas in our current society, family members often live great distances from one another. This certainly alters the time spent together physically, which may have tremendous impact on individual members as well as the relationship among the members. The distance may also change the psychological impact that family relations have on the family members. But despite how families have changed, they still have enormous influence on our lives and on all of our relationships.

This book explains some of the fundamental concepts found in Family Systems Theory. My intention is to encourage readers to use the concepts presented here to more fully understand how their original families' functioning, patterns, and processing have impacted them in the past, and continue to impact them in the here and now. Also, to recognize how their current relationships impact their extended family system.

This book is a user-friendly guide that explains how a family profoundly impacts its members in a myriad of ways, including:

- Influencing an individual's values and beliefs
- Influencing an individual's sense of self and identity in the world
- Teaching relational skills and emotional/rational responses

The more understanding and awareness you have of these influences, the more power you have to choose who and how you want to be, as well as how you want to relate to others.

As I was completing my graduate studies in counseling psychology in 1973, I was introduced to a *new* way of thinking. Up until the 1950s, most psychology was focused on the individual. By the time I was in graduate school, a new therapy was bursting onto the mental health scene: Family Therapy (Relationship Therapy), which was born out of Family Systems Theory. I became enthralled with this new paradigm, and have remained so throughout the years.

I was fortunate to be one of the early practitioners in this new field of marriage and family therapy, or *relationship* therapy. Now, many years later, having seen hundreds of individuals, couples and families, and teaching graduate courses in Marriage and Family Therapy, I am still fascinated with the study of family systems theory and relationship therapy.

This Labyrinth Called Life

As individuals, we travel this *Labyrinth Called Life*. As I imagine it, each person begins in the center of the labyrinth with one's birth mother and then one's family. We thus embark on our life's journey, traveling out from our families into the world.

Those of us who practice walking the Labyrinth of Life intentionally discover that in order to truly understand and know ourselves, it is important that we occasionally spiral back to our origins. This journey through the labyrinth is primarily a psychological journey. As we return to examine the beginning of our experiences with our families, our perspectives and understandings alter and deepen at different ages and stages of our lives. How a twenty-year-old understands her experience in her family is deeper and broader than when she was ten. And when this twenty-year-old is forty, her understanding of her family can be even greater, particularly if she chooses to traverse the labyrinth—circling in, circling out.

Those who never truly move outward do not have the perspective to understand their family's dynamics. Those who spiral outward but are unwilling to circle back periodically to experience, contemplate, and deepen their understanding often find themselves feeling disconnected. This person might experience not only being disconnected from family but also not being connected to self. Traversing the labyrinth of the family—moving inward, moving outward, returning, and leaving over the course of our lives—is essential for a true understanding of who we are.

For some, the family was and is experienced positively. Returning to the family either physically and/or emotionally/mentally is like returning to a precious touchstone that imbues us with strength and love. For others, the family was and is experienced negatively. To return physically and/or emotionally/mentally is like diving into the abyss. Most of us would prefer to avoid experiencing the abyss. But as many a wise person has implied, the only way to true healing is to be willing to plunge into the darkness of the abyss and attempt to find the light.

For most of us, the family has impacted us both positively and negatively. That seems to be part and parcel of the human experience.

I want to be clear; I am not advocating living in the past. I wholeheartedly believe that being in the present is what allows us to be fully alive and in touch with our power. However, one's past has a tremendous influence on one's present. I, therefore, advocate examining the past consciously, with intent, to give us knowledge and power in the present. If we avoid this conscious exploration, THE PAST will still be influencing us—we will simply be unconscious and unaware that it is doing so. Personally, I find conscious living to be preferable.

As is indicated in the table of contents, each chapter explains a concept pertinent to Family Systems Theory. At the end of each chapter is an inquiry that I encourage you to ponder. You may find it helpful to purchase a journal and record your responses to the questions. I also want to encourage you to consider discussing some of these inquires, as well as your thoughts and concerns, with family members.

*You Are Invited
to Journey*

The Labyrinth of Your Life

Circling In ~ Circling Out

May you accept this invitation and use this book as your guide.

Chapter One

Why Does It Matter?

The Importance of Understanding How
a Family System Operates

Every man is a quotation from all his ancestors.
RALPH WALDO EMERSON

*He who knows others is wise, but he who
knows himself is enlightened.*
LAO-TZU

I t may have been a dream.

I remember a man preaching from the pulpit with a strong booming voice proclaiming, "The greatest gift one can give to God is to know thyself."

Being an inquisitive and philosophical nine-year-old, I gave that statement much thought. I am sure it was just such *thinking* that brought me to the field of psychotherapy and, in particular, to the field of marriage and family therapy.

My paternal grandmother, known to us as "Bobba," started me on my journey to discovering myself. She delighted in the telling of family stories. It did not take me long to understand that it is, in fact, our stories and the messages in those real or imagined histories that help define how we think of ourselves, our lives, and the lives of others.

To "know thyself" is a great gift one can give to oneself, one's partner, and to one's children. It is impossible for us to know who we are as individuals without understanding our *family of origin*, our original family. Clearly, the relationships and events in the lives of children persist and define who they become as grown-ups.

Our stories help us to learn our family's values. They help us to know who and what is important. They help us to define who we are and our place in the world.

It is not only the stories we are told about who we are that influence us but also the stories we tell ourselves that define us; after all, we spend more time talking to ourselves than we do talking to others. Our present thoughts are influenced by our past experiences. We are "programmed" by what we see, hear, and experience.

The term *family values* has been used and abused in the current social and political scene. What I am referring to when I write of family values are the purposes, aspirations, and goals of the family. How is the family supporting its members? How is the family responding to and accomplishing the developmental tasks that often produce confusion and strife among the family members?

I think of a healthy family not as a family without problems but as a family that is resilient and uses its resources to move beyond those times of difficulty or crises.

Family crises often occur when the family is undergoing a *predictable* developmental change, such as marriage, adoption, birth, having a teenager, children leaving home, relocation, or the death of an elderly member.

Then there are crises that are experienced by the family that are not *predicted* or expected, such as the untimely death of a child, a spouse, or a parent. Some other situations that may create family crises are bankruptcy, hospitalization, financial difficulties, infidelity, divorce, child custody issues, remarriage, negotiating a blended family, separation due to military service or work, alcoholism, drug addiction, abuse, sexual identity issues, or suicide.

There's No Place Like Home

Family Systems Theory, unlike traditional psychoanalytic theory, focuses on the dynamics between family members rather than focusing on the psyches of each individual. Family Systems Theory is a relational model for understanding the human psyche. The relationship between family members, particularly the push and pull between family members for distance and closeness, is viewed as one of the major factors underlying human behavior.

Family Systems Theory considers not only the individuals living in a household but ALL of the family across time and generations, including extended family—grandparents, aunts, uncles, siblings, cousins. Most family therapists believe it is important to understand the family system across at least three generations, regardless of whether the persons are living or deceased, live nearby or far apart.

Individuals in a family share not only a history but also assumptions and beliefs about themselves, others, and how the world works. It is in our families that we learn how to relate to others in caring, nurturing, and supportive ways, and conversely, in ways that are hurtful, detrimental, and destructive.

Dorothy was right when she claims in *The Wizard of Oz*, "There's no place like home." This is true. You may have grown up in a loving, secure family that engendered loving and fond memories. Or you may have grown up in a chaotic and unsafe home. Thinking of "home" may bring up sad, hurt, even traumatic feelings. Nonetheless, *"there's no place like home."* It is the relationships we experience within our families that shape who we are, how we feel about ourselves, and how we attach and relate to others.

Family therapists believe that the power and influence of the relationships we have with other family members go beyond the grave. Neither distance nor death frees us from our family's influence. It is how one chooses to deal with one's family's influence that is crucial to one's well-being.

We have all experienced trauma.

What I mean by this is that I have yet to know anyone who has not had some life experience that has resulted in emotional suffering. Perhaps we have lost a loved one, or a beloved pet. Sometimes an injury or illness causes one to experience not only physical but also psychological trauma. Perhaps we experienced being bullied, or felt we were unjustly punished. I remember a childhood friend who got grounded for a month if she got anything less than an "A" on her report card.

The more fortunate among us have suffered less severe trauma, less often. Unfortunately, some have suffered intense and devastating emotional and psychological trauma that has an ongoing impact. These persons have suffered an event or events that have left them feeling emotionally overwhelmed, numb, profoundly anxious, often disconnected from self and others, and unsafe.

Unfortunately, there are many who have suffered severe emotional, physical, and verbal abuse from members of their families. Familial abuse, in my opinion, is the deepest, darkest, most devastating form of betrayal.

Whether an individual experiences repeated childhood trauma or a one-time traumatic event as an adult, feelings of shame and guilt often plague the trauma survivor. Trauma survivors describe sometimes experiencing difficulties in interpersonal relationships, particularly with those whom they are most intimate. Trauma survivors tend to suffer with depression, anxiety, and low self-esteem.

Those who have survived trauma have the capacity to recover from the wounds that may linger in their bodies, minds, and spirits. Healing these wounds takes time and commitment. In her inspiring memoir, *Never Tell,* Catherine McCall has written about her healing journey and the healing potential for sexual abuse survivors and their partners.

Healing from trauma wounds is a transformational journey that promotes the healing of the body, mind, and spirit. This journey is a relational journey that endeavors to heal the traumatized brain and attachment wounds, thus allowing for a balanced and positive sense of self and others. Understanding more about one's family dynamics can certainly help us to make new choices and navigate the present in healthier, more productive ways.

Family therapy operates from a *systems perspective*. That means that the family is viewed as a whole in which all individual members affect one another. Relationship interactions and patterns become the focus of exploring human problems. Thus, rather than the focus being on cause and effect (linear thinking), the focus is on the relationships and the patterns of connecting among the members of the system (circular thinking).

The Feedback Loop

Family Systems Theory began developing in the 1940s and '50s. Mathematicians and engineers during World War II designed machines that operated on the principle of a feedback loop. They used the idea that information can be fed back into a system, causing the system to respond to that information.

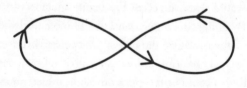

1.1. Feedback loop

So, how did this new theory effect the practice of psychotherapy?

In the early years of development of family systems theories, anthropologists and communication theorists studied how family members responded to one another in a *circular* modality, or feedback loop. Before systems theory and the understanding of circular causality, therapists instead worked from the idea of a linear causality.

The differences between linear and circular causality can be seen in the following example:

A mother brings her fifteen-year-old son, who has been skipping school and using drugs, to therapy. The therapist learns that the father recently lost his job. The son expresses that he is angry with the father because his father just "sits on the couch," making no effort to find work. This therapist hypothesizes that the son is expressing his anger toward the father by acting out or misbehaving (a linear causality). The father's behavior is thus causing the son's behavior. Father → Son or A → B

A systems therapist would not dismiss this hypothesis but would want to explore the presenting problem of the fifteen-year-old son acting out by attempting to understand the interdependence of all the relationships in the family. The therapist would consider how each person in the family is influencing the others.

The son has been presented by the family as the *identified patient*, the family member for whom therapy is sought. A family therapist sees the *family system* as the "patient." If I were the therapist, I would want to see all the family members in the first session. By doing so, I know that I would more likely be able to help the family identify the unhealthy or destructive relational patterns that are creating distress for individual members of the family. Thus, I could help them establish healthier, more productive patterns of relating, which would ultimately help the family resolve the "presenting problem" of the son's misbehaving.

I would ask that the entire family—the father, mother, son (fifteen) who is the identified patient, and the daughter (thirteen)—to come in for the first session. I always take a thorough family history. I begin with the nuclear family, which is the family as presented. In this case, that would be the mother, father, and two children. In taking a thorough family history, which includes at least three generations, I discover that in addition to the father having lost his job, the father's mother died recently in an automobile accident. The daughter shares that the mother has begun drinking more and that she is displaying more angry outbursts. The daughter describes that she is spending more time at home in her room, rather than doing things with her friends. The son is sullen, but freely expresses his anger toward both his parents.

I hypothesize that father is depressed, not only because he has lost his job and his mother but because he is also influenced by his son's acting out and his wife's increased drinking. The mother is depressed and angry with her husband and son. She is anxious about the family's financial security. The son, who is beginning to separate from the family (a normal developmental task), is angry and afraid. The daughter is so anxious about her father's well-being that she is afraid to leave the house. She is afraid that her family is "falling apart."

So instead of thinking of the problem as linear: Father → Son, the diagram changes to look like this (circular):

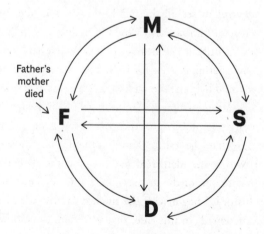

1.2. Circular causality

Viewing the family as a system shifts how presenting problems are explained, understood, and resolved.

It is not important to identify what may have started the problem. What is important is to identify the nonproductive/destructive ways of relating that are fueling the unhealthy patterns and then replace them with healthier, productive patterns of relating to one another.

As is illustrated by this example, the extended family, both living and deceased, influences what is going on with individual family members.

The system of a family must also be viewed in the broader context or the larger system. The cultural and societal impact on a family is extensive. Gender, class, race, sexual orientation, religion, and economic status influence an individual's values and beliefs. It is my experience that when the larger society is in transition or in crisis, the family and its individual members are more impacted than when the larger society is experiencing peace and calm. When a country is at war, for example, every individual and every family experiences the impact—of course, some more than others.

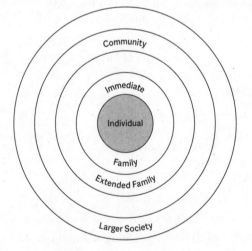

1.3. Viewing the family in a broader context

In all of my years working with individuals, couples, and families, I have never known a time when so many of my clients shared with me during the therapy hour how deeply impacted they are by the issues our country is currently experiencing. However, the primary focus of this book is on the nuclear family (parents—living together or separately—and offspring) and the extended family, rather than their community or the larger society and worldwide events.

Major Hypotheses of Family Systems Theory

In summary, Family Systems Theory is a philosophy of psychotherapeutic treatment and is used whether one is working with an individual, a couple, or a family.

Each person is considered a part of an interlocking relationship system that is constantly evolving and greater than the sum of its parts. No individual can be understood in isolation as he/she is embedded in a set of relationships.

Therefore:

- Behavior of an individual is as related to the interactional processes of the family as it is to the inner mental processes or emotional problems of the individual.
- A change in one member affects all other members and the family as a whole.

Families have a set of distinct properties, which includes:

- A set of rules
- Assigned and ascribed roles for its members
- An organizational structure
- Intricate overt and covert forms of communication
- Particular ways of negotiating and problem solving

The family is an organized social system in which individuals:

- Maintain a shared history
- Share an understanding about what it means to be a "family"
- Share perceptions about their family's identity
- Share assumptions about the world

Understanding our families—their patterns and connections, histories, and stories—frees us.

The purpose of understanding our families is not to blame and find fault. The purpose is to use our knowledge, awareness, and understanding to make conscious decisions as to how we WANT to be in the world. How do we WANT to feel, think, and behave?

Awareness and understanding equals power. The power to choose to change. The power to choose to think, feel, and behave in ways that allow us to flourish, not just exist and run on "autopilot."

Whatever the level of trauma we have experienced, knowledge, awareness, and understanding provide us with the power to choose to HEAL.

May you choose to HEAL. May you choose to get the help and support you need to do so.

Again, this book explains some of the fundamental concepts found in Family Systems Theory. The intention is to encourage readers to use the concepts presented to more fully understand how their family's functioning, patterns, and processing have impacted them in the past, and continue to impact them in the here and now.

May you use this knowledge to empower you to heal and create yourself and your life. I believe Sir Francis Bacon's quote from his book, *Meditations Sacrae and Human Philosophy* in 1597, **"Knowledge itself is power."**

Reflecting on Your Family of Origin

(the family in which you were raised)

1. What are some assumptions and beliefs that the individuals in your family believed about your family's identity? (Think about this from each family member's perspective.)

2. Identify some of the assumptions about the world that you were taught in your family. Do you share the same assumptions of how the world works that you were taught in your family?

3. What did you learn in your family about what it means to be a family? Do you now hold the same or a different definition about what it means to be a family?

Chapter Two

Who's in Charge?

Defining How a Family Structures
Itself for Good or Bad

All the world is a stage,
And all the men and women merely players:
They have their exits and their entrances
And one man in his time plays
Many parts . . .
WILLIAM SHAKESPEARE

Too many parents make life hard for their children by
trying, too zealously, to make it easy for them.
JOHANN WOLFGANG VON GOETHE

There are many ways to think about a family system. One
way is to analyze how a family *structures* itself. All families
have some kind of hierarchical structure, rules, and patterns of
interaction. The structure of a family defines these rules and
roles of its members, as well as patterns of functioning. The
structure of a family changes as the members age and as the family
experiences changes in the developmental stages of the individuals and the system as a whole.

Families are made up of subsystems. There may be a spousal or partner subsystem, a parental subsystem, a grandparent

subsystem, and a sibling subsystem. Each subsystem has an identity, particular functions, and specific patterns that are determined by the relationships between the subsystems.

Depicting the Family

One of the founders of Family Systems Theory, Murray Bowen, found it helpful when identifying family subsystems to diagram the family in a way that resembled constructing a family tree. This pictorial display of a family came to be known as a *genogram*. Genograms were developed and popularized in clinical settings by Monica McGoldrick and Randy Gerson through the publication of a book titled *Genograms in Family Assessment*. Therapists construct a genogram that allows them to look at a map or picture of a family and recognize important information about the family system without having to read through pages of notes on a family's history.

McGoldrick and Gerson devised symbols to indicate gender, as well as relationship patterns, including the reoccurring transgenerational patterns of behavior and hereditary tendencies. Their version of the genogram includes critical events such as births and deaths, as well as medical and mental health history.[1]

A basic genogram includes at least three generations. If a family that consisted of two parents (one female and one male) with two children (one female and one male) came to therapy, they would be represented in the following diagram as:

The grandparents: The First Generation

The parents: The Second Generation

The children: The Third Generation

I would inquire about the grandparents who are represented as The First Generation, requesting the personal details listed above, along with any other relevant information.

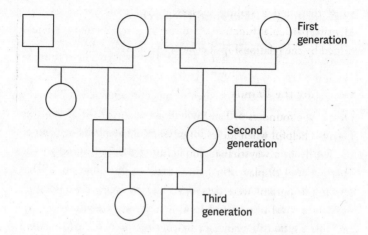

2.1. Basic three-generational genogram indicating gender

While the original genogram model used a circle to indicate a female, and a square to indicate a male person, many therapists have created their own symbols for transgendered and nonbinary individuals. For example: I use a circle inside a square to represent an individual born female who is now male or identifies as male.

2.2. Transgendered female to male

The genogram as a tool has been updated from its original format in many ways, and there have been many additions of representative symbols for individuals and relationship patterns over many years. I use genograms extensively throughout this book, to illustrate different examples of how family systems function both optimally and poorly. You will see many instances of these relationship pattern symbols as you move through the book.

Establishing the Parental Hierarchy

This chapter focuses primarily on families with children. Whether you are or are not a parent, I encourage you to think of your growing up in YOUR family of origin.

For a family raising children to function optimally, a hierarchy needs to exist. I cannot say enough about the importance of the hierarchy in the family—**the importance of parents being parents.**

Early in my career, I taught parenting classes. I would ask the participants to write down the answer to this question: "What feeling do you most want your child to feel?" I would then ask for a show of hands as to how many people wrote "happy." Almost always, about eighty percent of the participants raised their hands. I would then make a screeching noise that was my imitation of a loud, obnoxious buzzer, and I would proclaim, "Wrong answer!"

I would explain that the most important feeling a child can have is that of feeling *secure*. When a child feels secure, the child is then free to experience happiness, creativity, good self-worth, humor, and love. That feeling of security also enables the child to experience anger, disappointment, and sadness fully and freely and to express these feelings appropriately.

It is important to note that when children feel secure when they are young, they are more likely to develop secure, loving relationships later in life. I would tell those who answered with the word "happy" that one feels happy in momentary bursts. When we feel secure, we experience a deep and abiding knowing that sustains the essence of our being.

It is my belief that it is not only a parent's right but also the parent's *duty* to be in charge, so that the child knows that someone other than them is responsible for family life. Of course, the child feels most secure with parents who are caring for their feelings, wants, and needs.

A common challenge for a parent is to say "NO" and to stick with it. How many times in my life have I witnessed a parent saying "no" to a child two, three times before giving in to the child's demands? Literally—hundreds!

I was determined as a young parent to avoid this pitfall. And I think I did a really good job. That did not stop my sons from attempting to get me to overturn my "no" pronouncements. I humored myself by deciding that their commitment to "not taking no for an answer" was a part of their DNA. Nonetheless, I was determined not to succumb to their insistence. I, therefore, chose to live through temper tantrums, pouting, and their (very temporary) withdrawal of affection. But the payoff was worth it. They knew and I knew that I was in charge.

I have no memory of getting into verbal arguments with any of my three teenage sons. When I tell people this, they look both surprised and disbelieving. But it is true. By the time they became teenagers, they had learned that my "no" meant "no." My "no" was often delivered while having a conversation in the kitchen. I had a sign on the refrigerator that read: WHAT PART OF "NO" DON'T YOU UNDERSTAND?

So, the routine was:

1. A son would ask to do something that I was not willing to permit him to do.
2. I would say "no."
3. He would ask again, just to be sure.
4. I would hum, do a little dance, and point to the sign on the refrigerator.

Done. Discussion over. I smile just to think about it.

If children do not learn that "no" means "no" when they are two or three, then when they reach nine or fifteen it is much more difficult for them to accept.

I am sure my sons learned to not ask me some things when they knew the answer would be no. They either accepted that whatever it was they wanted was not going to happen, or they decided to do it without my knowing. I have to assume that did occur. After all, I was once a teenager. There are things my parents had no clue about my doing. I must assume that held true for my children as well.

Shifts in Hierarchical Functioning

Obviously, the hierarchy of a family changes as the children become adults. For instance, it is not uncommon for an adult child to "parent a parent" as that parent ages, particularly if the parent has ill health or cognitive decline.

In this kind of situation, parents with adult children sometimes are reluctant to honor the fact that they are no longer in charge, nor should they be. They still want the control, and believe that their children should do what they want them to do. It can be difficult in this circumstance for some adult children to release the belief that it is their role to please their parents. On the other side of the reaction spectrum, some teenagers and young adults rebel against parental authority as they attempt to assert control over their own lives.

Neither of these responses are healthy. Teens and young adults who rebel in order to break free of parental control often end up harming themselves in the process. Adult children who allow a parent to control their lives are not being true to themselves and are ignoring their own wants and needs for the sake of pleasing the parent.

I address healthier ways for individuals to gain autonomy as adults in later chapters.

Styles of Family Functioning

There are three basic styles of functioning that are most often used to describe how a family makes decisions and to describe the interactions between parents and children.

These are:

- **The Democratic Family**   The children have a voice. They have choices and their opinions are considered. However, the parents make the final decisions. The parents make rules that are clear, fair, and flexible. When the rules are broken, the parents follow through with age-appropriate consequences. Note: It is most helpful if the child knows the consequences beforehand.

- **The Autocratic Family**   The children do not have a voice. The parents set rules that may or may not be fair or clear. When the rules are broken, the parents follow through with consequences. However, quite often, the parents set forth consequences or punishments that are unfair and unrelated to the "crime."

- **The Permissive Family**   Quite often the children rule the household. Very few rules exist. If a child does break a rule, there are likely to be no consequences of meaning to the child.

In my experience, autocratic families and permissive families are more likely to seek therapy for problems dealing with the children than democratic families. Democratic families are not immune to needing family therapy. However, the presenting problem is generally not related to the issue of "who's in charge." The exception to this may be during a time of transition; for example, when a child is an adolescent and is challenging the "rules."

When families come into therapy because of a child's acting out or misbehaving in some way, we often discover that the problem is ultimately because the parents are not doing an adequate job of being in charge of the family. This is equally true in families where the parents have almost no rules or consequences and those families that have many rules and punishments.

Having a lot of rules for your child and punishing them frequently does not make you a parent who provides the child with a sense of security and well-being. We all tend to feel more secure when those who are supposed to be in charge are responsible, set reasonable limits and boundaries, and are people we know care about our well-being. This is true whether we are children in a family or citizens in a nation.

Boundaries and Subsystems

In a family with young children, it is important that there is a clear hierarchal structure delineating the family's subsystems. The parental subsystem must always be the executive subsystem.

Boundaries function to delineate the subsystems and the individuals in the subsystems. Each subsystem has defined functions and defined patterns of relating within and between the subsystems.

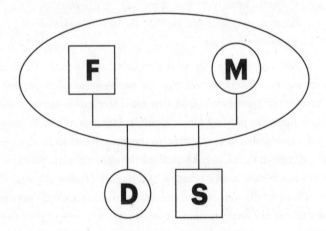

2.3. Parental subsystem

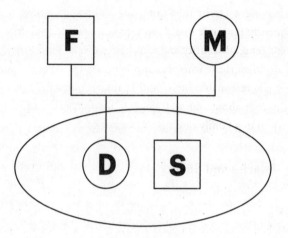

2.4. Sibling subsystem

It is important that appropriate boundaries exist between the subsystems. Parents must be in charge. It is optimal if parents can support each other. This holds true even if the parents are divorced or do not live together.

Side note: This would not be true if one parent is abusing a child. It is the obligation of parents to provide safety for their children. If one parent is abusing a child, the other parent needs to take action to provide safety for the child. In some states this is a legal requirement. There are states in which the non-abusive parent is held accountable for the abuse as well as the parent perpetrating the abuse.

The boundaries between the subsystems and within a subsystem are critical to the health of the family system. Boundaries within a family are defined in the traditional family therapy literature as either clear, rigid, or diffuse.

Clear boundaries are considered ideal. Clear boundaries are firm as well as flexible. The individual members of the family are nurtured and supported and allowed appropriate autonomy (depending upon the age of the individuals).

In a family that has rigid boundaries, the members are disengaged. They experience isolation from one another. They are so focused on their own issues that they are not available to respond and support one another. The phrases "Do it yourself" and "Don't bother me" are commonly heard. Families with rigid boundaries are often closed off to the rest of the world.

Families that have diffuse boundaries are characterized by enmeshed relationships. Everybody is into everybody's business. One or both parents may be overly involved and overly accessible to their children. The spousal subsystem gets swallowed into the parental subsystem, as the parents' lives revolve primarily around the children. The spousal unit is not given adequate attention and can suffer tremendously. Children rely too much on the parents and are stifled in becoming independent and autonomous.

Often problems experienced in a family are due to there being a diffuse boundary in which there is a cross-generation coalition. For example, a mother and teenage daughter are exceptionally close and tend to leave the father out of discussions and activities. He may attempt to have more interaction with the mother by arguing about mundane issues. Or he may go outside of the marriage to get his intimacy needs met, whether that is on the golf course with his buddies or with a woman at work. Again, the systems therapist is not as interested in attempting to identify "why" the problem started as in what patterns keep it going. In this family, the distance experienced by the couple IS the issue.

One of the early family systems therapists, Salvador Minuchin, introduced a technique called family mapping to illustrate hierarchy and boundaries between individuals and subsystems. It was his position that clear boundaries between subsystems help ensure the security and well-being of the family as a whole.[2]

Boundaries are represented as:

DIFFUSE - - - - - - - - - - - - (enmeshed relationships)
RIGID — — — — — — — — — (disengaged-distant)
CLEAR - — - — - — - — - — (clear but flexible)

2.5. Representation of boundaries

The family in which the mother and teenage daughter are exceptionally close, and the father is distant, would look like this at the time they entered therapy:

Rigid boundary between M and F
Rigid boundary between F and D
Diffuse boundary between M and D

2.6. Family boundary 1

The goal of therapy would be to help the parents reconnect in a healthy way and allow the daughter to have access to both parents while becoming a more independent, autonomous adult. This would be represented in the following family map:

Clear boundary between M and F
Clear boundary between F and D
Clear boundary between M and D

2.7. Family boundary 2

In some families, the closeness between a mother and daughter is in no way related to distance between the parental couple. The couple's relationship may not be experiencing any issues, and the closeness between mother and daughter may or may not be a problem in and of itself. If the closeness of their relationship is negatively affecting any of the individuals or relationships in the family, then it is a problem. It may be that the daughter is being held back from a healthy developmental journey, or that another sibling feels neglected or "less than."

Working Toward Clear Boundaries

There are times when a child is the one who wants and works to create clear, healthy boundaries. We see this most often with teenagers.

When I was sixteen, my father fell off a roof and broke almost every bone on the left side of his body below his neck. He was unable to drive for months. My mother did not drive, so at sixteen I became the primary driver. It became my responsibility to chauffeur my younger brother and sister to and from places, to drive my mother to and from the hospital, and to run family errands.

I was elevated in the hierarchy of my family to the parental subsystem by necessity. I felt that this was more responsibility than I wished to have.

After several months, I insisted that my mother get her driver's license; she agreed. The first time I took her to practice driving on a nearby country road, a golden retriever ran in front of the car. She hit the dog, and he died instantly. The dog's owner and I attempted to reassure my mother that it was not her fault; no one could have avoided hitting the dog. She remained hysterical and proclaimed that she was never going to get behind the wheel again!

At first, I felt sad and discouraged. However, it did not take long before I resolved that this situation could not continue to exist.

I waited a few days before walking into the kitchen with car keys in hand. I said firmly and calmly, "It is time for us to take a drive."

Silence. My mother looked like a deer in headlights. "Come on," I coaxed. She did, and within a few weeks obtained her driver's license. I was able to go back to being a teenager, resuming my place in the child subsystem!

Generational boundary issues not only occur between a parent and child but often involve other members of the extended family. Another example of a cross-generational boundary issue involves grandparents. In some situations, a grandparent may have more authority and control over grandchildren than a parent. Thus, when the parent attempts to "parent," the child ignores the parent and goes to the grandparent for structure. Grandparents can undermine parents. This often occurs by collusion between the grandparent and grandchild through indulgence. Neither of these situations are detrimental if they happen infrequently and are not ongoing patterns. (Spoken as an adoring grandmother—guilty!)

Transforming Unhealthy Rigid Boundaries

One of the miracle cures I experienced when working with a family involved a mother and teenage son who had, over time, developed a rigid boundary between them due to the son not having access to his mother in the way that he needed at his developmental stage.

The parents had divorced when the son was about ten years old. At the time of the parents' divorce, another son was living in the home, but the older son had graduated and gone away to college. The younger son was responsible and self-sufficient; however, the family was referred to me because he was exhibiting signs of depression. He was also getting low grades in several courses—something that had never occurred before now, his senior year in high school.

The mother had a very stressful and demanding job as a CEO in a large corporation. She worked late most nights. She had recently started dating a man in another state, and often traveled on the weekends to be with her boyfriend. I saw the mother and son together for several sessions so that I could hear the problem from each of their points of view. I also wanted to get a family history. I then met individually with each one. The son shared that he was happy for his mother to have a boyfriend and that he liked the man. I believed he was sincere.

As I listened intently to the young man, I realized he was *missing* his mother. So, I hypothesized to them during the next family session that the son needed more "mothering" before he left for college in the fall. They both sat looking at me like I had lost my mind. But I stayed with my hypothesis. I then asked them if they were willing to try an experiment. They both agreed. I asked the mother to make a promise to her son that she would come home early enough for them to have dinner together two nights a week. The son was so excited by this idea that he offered to fix the dinner! So, they planned a menu, the mother bought the groceries, and the son or the two of them together fixed the meals. When I saw them two weeks later, the son was markedly less depressed. When I saw them four weeks after *that*, the son's grades were back on track.

What would have happened if the son had gone for individual therapy where his depression became the focus rather than the family relationship?! Often, well-meaning parents take their children for individual therapy when family therapy is what is truly needed. Working with children individually has its place and can be helpful, AS LONG AS the family relationships are not neglected.

Boundaries and the Outside World

Boundaries also exist between the family and the outside world. A family with open boundaries to the outside world means that the individuals are free to go outside and be themselves. It also means that the family is open to welcoming new ideas as well as other people into the world of the family.

A family with open boundaries to the outside world is usually considered healthy and positive. However, I have witnessed families where the boundaries were so open that one or more members of the family suffered. This most often occurs when a family has very few boundaries with the outside world. An example of this is a family that has an "open door" policy. In this situation, people are constantly coming and going. Individual privacy is not respected, or is minimal. Chaos is the norm.

Conversely, a closed family system is shut off from the world. A closed system is resistant to change. I have never witnessed a closed system that did not have at least one of its members suffering profoundly and deeply. Closed family systems usually exist because the outside world seems threatening in some way. Perhaps the family is hiding a secret of physical or sexual abuse, mental illness, or substance abuse.

All this to say: a clear—not a diffuse or rigid—boundary between the family and the outside world is optimal. A clear boundary still allows for openness and is considered to be optimal for a healthy and well-functioning family.

Change in Subsystems

The life of a family changes over time. Theories of family development note transition points in a family's life cycle that require structural changes so that a family will remain functional. Marriage, the birth of a child, children entering school, adolescence, and children leaving home are among these expected transitions.

Other challenges, as well as an unexpected crisis, may require a change in a family's way of structuring itself. Death of a family member, especially an unexpected and untimely death, can throw a family into crisis and chaos. Divorce, unemployment, illness, incarceration, economic forces, and war are some of the factors that necessitate change in how a family operates and structures itself.

Divorce creates a cascade of changes in the subsystems, which in turn changes functions and relationship patterns for not only the couple but also the entire family. If the divorced couple has children and one or both remarry, then reorganizing the family structure in regard to how the family operates becomes even more complicated.

In my practice, I see two major pitfalls presented over and over in stepfamilies. The first one occurs when the newly married couple attempts to function in their blended family as though they are an *intact* nuclear family. An intact nuclear family is one in which there are two married adults with their offspring living in the same household or as one unit. But unless the children are very young, a blended family will not usually be successful in adopting the previous roles, rules, functioning, and expectations that they had in their nuclear families. Blended families need to create a new and different structure. The intact, nuclear family paradigm will not work!

The second difficulty I typically see happens when a stepparent does not understand that they will have a different relationship with their stepchildren than does the original parent. This has so many implications that I cannot begin to cover them in this book. Fortunately, there are many good books, blogs, and podcasts available regarding stepparenting. But the one guideline I want to emphasize is that the original parent needs to be the *primary* parent of their biological children, particularly when teenagers are present in the newly formed family.

Under-functioning and Over-functioning

At times circumstances create an over-functioning and an under-functioning parental subsystem. If one parent has an accident or becomes ill, the other parent will need to over-function to keep the family operating as best it can. There are times when a family system casts an individual in the role of the one who over-functions or under-functions. Generally, the mother tends to be cast in (and readily accepts) the role of the person who over-functions. The over-functioning parent tends to be over-involved as well. The over-involved parent is often described as a *helicopter parent*, always hovering over the child.

Over-functioning persons may take on way too much responsibility for the functioning of the family. They often think it is their job to take care of others even when it is not necessary and often not healthy. They tend to neglect their own wants and needs and are in danger of emotional and physical illness. If they are over-involved as well as over-functioning, they worry excessively about everyone and everything. They therefore act in ways that others experience as controlling or overbearing.

The person in the under-functioning role assumes less responsibility for the whole. Sometimes this person acts irresponsibly and indifferently. This person may be emotionally distant and unavailable.

When family members take on the roles of under-functioning and over-functioning to the extreme, everyone pays a price.

Over-functioning and under-functioning appear in many different ways in the family. The most obvious would be when there is one person who is responsible for the family financially, as well as running the household and taking care of the children, while the other parent goes about the day doing what they want without regard to the needs of the family.

I am thinking of a family in which the father went to a job during the day, stopped by the grocery store on the way home to get groceries to prepare the evening's dinner, checked the children's homework, and then put them to bed. Meanwhile, his spouse spent her day at the country club playing tennis or bridge. She would have a few drinks before coming home when the children got home from school. She would then take a nap and get up in time to have dinner with the family. After dinner, she would begin drinking again. This is clearly an example of an over-functioning parent (the father) and an under-functioning parent (the mother).

There are situations, however, when over-functioning and under-functioning are not as clear. I've seen many families where both parents participate fully in the financial aspect of providing for the family and in maintaining their residence, but only one of the parents takes on the responsibilities that involve the children. In single-parent families, this is always the case, but it also occurs in two-parent families. So, in this situation, both individuals are functioning and may be high functioning. However, only one is over-functioning concerning parenting responsibilities, while the other is under-functioning, taking very little responsibility for childcare.

I have seen many couples whose presenting problem in marriage therapy is that the over-functioning person feels resentful, hurt, and often alone. It is almost always true that the over-functioning partner brings in the under-functioning partner for marriage counseling. The over-functioning person usually describes their partner as "lazy" or self-centered. And this may well be the case. There are situations when the under-functioning person is actually doing the best they can do at the present time; the under-functioning person may be in the throes of deep grief, or may have a mental illness. And, then again, this person may be "lazy" or self-centered.

The more the spousal/parental subsystem can take on a relationship of equality, the healthier the family system will be.

In single-parent families, the parent must be mindful of not assigning to a child a parental role that denies the child the freedom to be a child. It is also important that the single parent be mindful to adequately take care of herself/himself and to avoid being *overly* involved when unnecessary.

Over-functioning is unavoidable at times, but must be managed and mitigated wherever possible in order to maintain a healthy balance for all family members.

Roles and Rules

Another way the family structures itself is by defining roles that the individual members assume. Some families come to therapy because of issues involving these roles and their associated responsibilities. It is not unusual for a newly formed couple to come in to discuss how they will manage the roles demanded of them. Who is the wage earner? Who handles the finances? Who is responsible for cooking and cleaning? Who is responsible for childcare? Who is the social scheduler? Who provides emotional support? These jobs need to be performed so that the family can function.

At times, the jobs required of family members and the roles that family members play are synonymous. The individual members become identified by their job/role: The wage-earner. The cook. The caretaker. The fixer.

In other families, there is no role associated with the individual performing a job. More than one individual may support the family financially. More than one individual prepares meals and cleans the house. More than one individual takes care of the children.

Jobs and roles are not synonymous. When jobs and roles are synonymous, it is not particularly detrimental. It may become detrimental, however, if an individual begins to feel trapped or burdened to the point of physical or emotional distress or illness.

One's role in a family may not be related to a particular job that needs doing. The role may fulfill a more relational or emotional need in the family. For example, someone may take on the role of the compassionate advisor. If a member of the family has a problem, they seek out the person who has this role.

Role ascription may be related to gender or birth order. The youngest female may be expected to take care of the parents in their elder years. This would be an example of a role that is prescribed at birth, a role that is "stamped on the forehead," so to speak. Another example is that of a son born into a family in which generations of the males have been lawyers. He is cast as the next lawyer to manage the family law firm.

Children are often cast in the role as "the smart one," "the pretty one," "the funny one," etc. When a role becomes rigid, it becomes a problem. If only one son is allowed to be the hero, and he absolutely must be the hero, then dysfunction can be a result. The same goes for the scapegoat, the caregiver, the comedian, and so on. If a family is flexible and individuals can move in and out of their assigned roles, then there is less likely to be a situation in which one or more of the family members suffer.

To sum up the most important parts of this chapter:

A healthy family system takes care of the individuals in the family. An unhealthy family system sacrifices the individual(s) to take care of the system.

- The structure of a family system is important to the health of the members of the system.
- It is important that in a family with children there is a hierarchy, with a responsible subsystem in charge. Usually, this is a parent or parents.

- A healthy family has clear boundaries that exist between the subsystems, and these boundaries are firm and flexible.
- A healthy family does not assign rigid roles in which individuals get stuck and, therefore, suffer.
- A healthy family encourages its members to have a healthy interaction with the world around them.

Always remember that a family is more than individuals who share physical space. These individuals share psychological space as well, which is important to take into account in all family interactions.

Identifying Family Structure

First, think of the following questions in relationship to your family of origin, the family into which you were born and raised. Then go back and respond in relationship to your current family.

How are they similar/different? Do you know what the family structure was like for your parents when they were children? I invite you to be aware of your feelings as you explore the answers to these questions.

Structure and Hierarchy

1. If you were/are in a single-parent family, did/do one or more children take on an adult role?

2. If a grandparent was/is living in the home, was/is there ever confusion about who was/is in control?

3. Were/are the parents united or divided?

4. Who determined(s) the emotional climate of the family? (I am thinking of the saying, "There ain't nobody happy unless Momma's happy.")

5. What kind of messages did/do you get about WHO in the family should be in control?

Over-involved or Under-involved

1. Was/is at least one parent over-involved with at least one child?

2. Was/is one or more parent peripheral or under-involved?

Styles of Functioning

1. What style did/do the parents use in relating to the children?

   - **Democratic** Children have a voice. They have choices and their opinions are considered. However, the parents make the final decision. The rules are clear and flexible. When the rules are broken, the parents follow through with age-appropriate consequences.
   - **Autocratic** The parents set the rules. The rules are clear and inflexible. When the rules are broken, the parents follow through with the consequences. Often the parents set forth a punishment that is unfair and unrelated to the "crime."
   - **Permissive** Very few rules, child-focused. When a child does break a rule there is often no consequence of importance.

2. Was/is the discipline fair and consistent? Inconsistent? Nonexistent? Overly severe?

3. Was/is more attention given to undesirable (bad) behavior or desirable (good) behavior?

4. Was/is more attention given to positive reinforcers (rewarding desirable behavior) or negative reinforcers (punishing bad behavior)?

5. Do you ever catch yourself doing things much like another member of your family of origin? Who would you say was the most influential model in the development of your behavioral style?

6. As a child, how did you punish or reward your parents? What was the most effective punishment? Do you still find yourself using these sources of reinforcement and punishment with your parents? Your partner? Your children?

Having pondered these questions, I encourage you to think of what you might want to do differently or change in the here and now.

Chapter Three

Is It Safe to Say What You Mean and to Mean What You Say?

Identifying Communication Roles, Rules, Patterns, and Possibilities

In our family, an experience was not finished, not truly experienced, until written down and shared with another.

ANNE MORROW LINDBERGH

I have often found myself amused when either a couple or a family with a teenager comes in for therapy and states, "We just don't communicate."

Paul Watzlawick was an Austrian-American family therapist, psychologist, communication theorist, and philosopher. He, along with Don Jackson and others, provided the field of systems theory with important information regarding the subject of communication.

First of all, according to Watzlawick et al.:

- One cannot NOT communicate.
- Also, an individual cannot not behave.
- All behavior is communication on some level.[1]

One of the early family therapists, Virginia Satir, wrote in 1972: "I see communication as a huge umbrella that covers and affects all that goes on between human beings. Once a human being has arrived on this earth, communication is the largest single factor determining what kinds of relationships she or he makes with others and what happens to each in the world. How we manage survival, how we develop intimacy, how productive we are, how we make sense, how we connect with our own divinity—all depend largely on our communication skills."[2]

It is a commonly held belief among mental health professionals that if one is not allowed to have their feelings and to express those feelings appropriately that one's self-esteem is at risk. Successful relationships are dependent on good communication and problem-solving skills.

Most of us became aware very early in our lives that communication is delivered both *verbally* and *non-verbally*. We know that voice tone, inflection, gestures, body language, changes in breathing, and facial expressions actually convey more than the words themselves. Many of us grew up hearing expressions such as "Actions speak louder than words" and "Do as I say, not as I do."

I have also observed that we tend to *not* hear ourselves. We know what words we are saying, but we do not know what message we are sending. We often imply non-verbally our disappointments, our anger, and our critical judgment of the other.

Virginia Satir described communication "roles" that individuals in a family often adopt. In each of these roles, some aspect of emotional experience is denied, either for the sender or the receiver of the message.

These are the roles Satir described:

- **Placater** The person who desires to please others at all costs. Often embodies weakness and passivity.
- **Blamer** The individual who is very judgmental, disagreeable, and is quick to blame others.

- **Superreasonable** The extremely logical individual who shies away from feeling.
- **Irrelevant** The individual who uses distracting behaviors, without consideration for others, in the process of communication.
- **Congruent** The individual whose communication is consistent in word and feeling.[3]

Another category I would add is the person who ALWAYS has to be right.

I often ask the question, "Would you rather be right or happy?" It seems many people choose, at times without awareness, to remain unhappy and to hold on tight to the concept of being *right*.

Most of us recognize these styles of communicators. Of course, the ideal would be for all of us to be *congruent* communicators. To be a congruent communicator, one needs to be able to identify and communicate one's own thoughts and feelings as well as be able to identify and hear the thoughts and feelings of the other.

When the verbal message and the non-verbal message are not congruent, the receiver of the message may experience tension. At times, this incongruence may even be crazy-making.

For example: A father says to a child in an angry tone with a scowl on his face, "I love you." The verbal message and non-verbal message being incongruent may confuse, even disorient the child. If this incongruent communication style is experienced repeatedly, the child may become seriously emotionally damaged.

Communication is about *sending* and *receiving* messages. Listening is crucial. Whether or not family members are attentive—not only to the content but to the feelings underlying the message of the sender—determines the degree to which intimacy can be experienced. The level of intimacy is directly related to the safety an individual experiences in the relationship.

Is it safe to share who I really am? How I really feel?

Will you be honest and truthful with me?

Individuals often equate sex with intimacy. In fact, true intimacy is directly related to how safe one feels in the relationship. The degree to which an individual experiences safety impacts his degree of satisfaction in the relationship and his own self-esteem.

One of my father's favorite sayings was, "Say what you mean, and mean what you say." I've always believed this to be a really good rule to live by. The problem is, others do not always appreciate this philosophy. There are times they do not want to hear what I have to say. They are more comfortable with the rule, "If you can't say anything nice, don't say anything at all." The latter quote can be useful, particularly when it comes to being judgmental or critical about something relatively unimportant. For example, a woman who offers unsolicited comments to her friend that the dress she is wearing is not flattering. What's the point? She's wearing it. She did not ask for this opinion. So, unless she does, don't offer it!

Often individuals do not share thoughts and feelings that are important to them because they are afraid they will upset the other person or that they will be rejected. I do believe that to say what you mean and to mean what you say takes good self-esteem. Meaning what you say and saying what you mean also helps to build good self-esteem. Being in a family that not only allows for this but also encourages it can be a positive experience for the members of this family. If done in an honest, open, and considerate way, saying what you mean and meaning what you say can offer an opportunity for personal growth as well as enhancing relationships. However, if it is used to hurt or diminish others, then negative results will occur personally and relationally.

When working with a couple or a family, it is often easy to assess how safe and secure the members in the family feel simply by asking and observing the answer to this question, "Do you each feel it is safe to share your thoughts and feelings?"

As they respond, I listen to their words, their tone of voice, and observe their non-verbal behavior. An individual may answer "yes" to the question; however, this person may look down and speak in a barely audible voice. The verbal and non-verbal response is not congruent. The lack of congruency would be a clue that, in fact, the individual does not feel safe to share honest thoughts and feelings.

Practicing Healthy Communication in the Family

It is in our families that we have the greatest opportunity to experience intimate or *connecting* communication. Much of our communication, once we enter school, takes place outside of our families. These outside encounters impact our sense of ourselves as well, but generally not to the degree that does our family.

Both in and out of the family we engage in communication that is informational, confrontational, motivational, and intimate. We may problem-solve, "cuss," and discuss. Hopefully we experience closeness and intimacy. It is within our FAMILIES that the best opportunity is provided for us to learn how to connect and maintain connectedness. It is in our families where we can, hopefully, share our hopes, our dreams, our fears, our sadness, and our joy. It is where we listen and respond to one another at many different levels. If a family can do this well, the family members are more likely to experience safety and a positive sense of well-being.

Every family has a set of rules regarding accepted and unaccepted ways of communicating, which is passed on to its members. The rule "Children are to be seen and not heard" is an example of one that discourages healthy communication. There is healthy and unhealthy communication. Unhealthy communication includes destructive communication. If the person expressing himself intends to hurt the other person or wishes to elicit guilt in the other person, that would be considered destructive communication. Some communication practices are almost always destructive.

Destructive Communication Practices, or Communication Practices Guaranteed to RUIN Relationships

- **Blaming** "It's your fault the dog got out." Most of us have met a person who is most always on the defensive. My experience is that individuals who communicate from this defensive posture are either not willing to take responsibility or are afraid of being chastised themselves (or both). So they operate from the position of, "I'll blame you before you blame me." Or they blame the other as a response to being questioned if they feel their sense of self is under attack.

- **Labeling** "You're a jock. You are not smart enough to do that job." If you have ever had a label applied to you and then a conclusion drawn about you because of the label, you know how unfair that feels. My now-white hair was once blond. I cannot tell you how many times I was referred to as a "dumb" or "ditzy" blond by people who did not know me. Fortunately, I knew my IQ was higher than most of theirs and was able to walk away emotionally unscathed, but momentarily rattled nonetheless. Often in families children are labeled "the smart one," "the pretty one," "the clown," "the good one," "the black sheep," etc.

- **Name-calling** "You are such an idiot." Name-calling seems more and more common in conversations between family members who show up in my practice. I guess it is more acceptable and commonplace in our society. The phrases "You bitch" and "You asshole" are not even censored on television any more. If your intention is to hurt the listener, then name-calling may work. If your intention is to be heard and understood, then name-calling is destructive and detrimental to your attaining that goal.

- **Accusing** "You left the gate open on purpose." Most of the time when an individual adopts an "accusing" communication style, they are actually assigning a hypothetical reason as to why the other did what they did. In the example above, "You left the gate open . . ." may be fact or not. It is the ". . . on purpose" that is the most damaging to the communication. Jumping to conclusions about another's actions is dangerous business when it comes to important relationships.

- **Put-downs** "Really? You never do it right." "Will you ever learn how to use that remote?" In the past decade I have observed that there is one word that seems to rule the tactic of put-downs. That word, spoken with disgust, is "Really?" (The implication being the other is doing or saying something wrong.)

- **Threatening** "The next time you do that, I am leaving." Making threats can be deadly to relationships. If the threats are *idle threats* (have no real consequences attached to them), then they are often ignored. Idle threats that are continuous will, however, create an unsafe space for trust and open, honest communication.

- **Mind-reading** "I know you did this to get back at me." Mind-reading can look a lot like accusing when it has to do with making assumptions about the other's intentions. I have always appreciated the old saying that goes something like: "When you assume, you make an _ass_ out of _u_ and _me_."

- **Demanding** "Mow the grass, now." Demanding usually carries a threat with it. "It's my way or the highway." "You do this or else!" The "or else" may be a withdrawal of affection or a "tit for tat." Example: "If you don't mow the grass today, then I am not going with you to the party tonight."

- **Constant Complaining** "I hate the way you drive." (Spoken each time entering the car before even getting out of the garage.) Constant complaining is a real buzz kill. The persons complaining rarely get what they want by complaining. So, all that they really accomplish is creating distance in the relationship, which makes it less likely that positive communication can occur.

- **Withholding** "I am not going to tell you why I am upset." It is much more likely that someone with a withholder style of communication would say nothing. I have seen many couples who come for therapy because one partner is so frustrated and angry that their partner withholds. A withholder may be doing so to punish their partner. It is just as likely to be a learned response stemming from the withholder's history.

- **Judging** "There is something wrong with you." (Spoken with complete disdain.) Judging behavior is very different from expressing judgment of a person. Let me set a scenario for the example above. A mother just witnessed her husband yelling viciously at their son. Instead of attacking her husband's personhood, she could have said, "I am very distressed that you so viciously yelled at our son. It makes me angry and sad. I am concerned about how your yelling affects him. I want you to do what it takes to try and understand why you get so angry and resort to yelling." Note: Individuals who have spent much of their childhood being chastised and judged by parents and other authority figures often experience low self-esteem.

- **Defensiveness** "I am not going to listen to you." Most of the previous destructive communication styles are also defensive postures. The reason this is listed separately is because it is so common and often stands alone. The individuals who adopt this communication style may or may not engage in the previously listed styles. These individuals often stay distant from others at a feeling level. When I picture them, they are walking around with "their dukes up." (This is an old slang phrase that means putting up your fists to be ready for a fight.) The individuals who frequently use this style of communication are usually terrified of being vulnerable.
- **Dismissiveness** "I don't care what you have to say." This communication style is common to the individuals who feel the need to always be "right." When you are someone who has been on the receiving end of dismissiveness, you may feel unimportant and unworthy. As is true of the other styles listed, it is destructive not only to having good communication with those with whom you are in relationship but also to the psyche of those persons on the receiving end.
- **Passive-aggressive** "I will do it after work." (With no intention of follow-through, i.e., saying what you think the other person wants to hear to shut them up.) If this communication style is frequent in a relationship, trust will be completely undermined.
- **Lying** "I never let the dog out of the house." (Even when you did!) As it is with passive-aggressive communication, lying undermines trust. In a relationship without trust, individuals will have too much fear to be open and honest, thus making closeness and openness impossible.

Healthy families where such destructive communication is infrequent or nonexistent provide a constructive context for openly sharing one's experiences and feelings. Disagreements are allowed and negotiation is encouraged.

In some families, there are rules about what can be talked about. What we communicate verbally is often categorized as being *topic-related, personal, and relational*. It is in the family where we most often share our personal selves and focus on relationship issues, but within families, there are often spoken and/or unspoken rules surrounding these conversations.

I was very fortunate to grow up in a family that encouraged many interesting discussions around the dinner table. As I recall these fabulous talks, they were almost always topic-related. We discussed external circumstances, including daily activities, history, religion, and politics. We had many enlivening intellectual debates. This was great fun, and I learned that we could agree to disagree and still appreciate and enjoy one another in this experience. It wasn't until I was an adult that I realized having this experience with my family at the dinner table was highly unusual.

One of the assessments I sometimes use when working with clients to ascertain the closeness and safety of communication in their families is to ask them to describe a typical mealtime experience. I think of one adult client who was the youngest of ten children. He would come home from school and get so involved with whatever he was doing that he would miss supper. No one called him or went to get him. When he got hungry he would go into the kitchen to discover that supper was over and that there was no food left for him. He would cry, some of his older siblings would make fun of him, and he would go to bed hungry. This happened often.

Just by hearing about his experience around his family's mealtime helped me to understand why he had such low self-esteem and was so distrusting of others.

Some of the questions I ask about family mealtime experiences are:

- Do they eat separately or together?
- Do they have conversations while eating?
- Who does the talking?
- What are the conversations generally about?
- Do they experience mealtimes as positive or negative? Why?

As wonderful as I think my family's dinner conversations were, the conversations were rarely about us personally or relationally (as in our relationships to one another within the family). We were never told that personal or relational conversations were off limits, but this was an "implied" rule that we certainly adhered to, nonetheless. We could share personal information, like "I made an A on the history test." But this sharing of personal information rarely went beyond information into "feelings." I do not remember ever hearing anything like, "I am so sad that I misspelled two words on the spelling test today."

Some families do not allow for the expression of feelings at all. There are also families in which the unspoken rule is that females can express feelings, but not males. Or that anger may be expressed, but not sadness. Either way, every family has a set of spoken and unspoken rules that govern communication.

An Issue or a Problem?

When it comes to communication, we often tend to classify our struggles as "problems." As a young therapist, I was sometimes confused when a couple or a family would come in and present what they called "A PROBLEM." I finally realized that I made a distinction between an issue and a problem.

We all have issues. Life presents issues frequently. An issue may become a problem if it is avoided, or is recurrent and not dealt with in a way that is satisfactory to the persons involved. Working through issues successfully in relationships is essential for the well-being of the individuals and their relationships.

Let me give you an example: A young couple, married for three years, came in for couple therapy. They were obviously agitated and angry at each other. The wife, crying, began, "We have only been married three years, and I feel neglected. He takes me for granted. Every day when he comes home from work we get into a fight. The other night he actually kicked the dog. That's when I called to make the appointment with you. I always end up crying. We each go to our corners and sulk. We eat dinner silently and I go to the bedroom and read, and he stays in the family room and watches TV. I'm sick of it! Maybe we should just get divorced!"

I turn to the husband without saying a word. He begins, "I'm sick of it, too! I have a demanding job and a boss that I hate. The guy is a real jerk. Isn't your home supposed to be a refuge? I come home and as soon as I walk in the door, she starts in." He continues, "The other night she was starting in with her nonsensical babble and the dog ran up and jumped on me and I snapped. Yes, I pushed the dog out of the way with my foot. I did not 'kick' him. I pushed him away, really. But I was yelling and angry. Then, of course, she went nuts! That's when I agreed to see a marriage counselor."

PROBLEM: The couple is fighting. Both are feeling unhappy and distant.

ISSUES that have been avoided or unsatisfactorily resolved that birthed The Problem:

- **Issue #1** The husband obviously needs a way to release his frustration with his job and anger toward his boss. (Note: The husband did continue to do some individual work around dealing with his boss and job with a career counselor. But at this point in the couple therapy, it was important that his anger and frustration did not infringe on the husband-and-wife relationship.)

- **Issue #2** The wife's eagerness to engage with her husband when he gets home is experienced as a curse rather than a blessing. (The wife is a homemaker in a new neighborhood. She spends most of the day at home alone.)
- **Issue #3** The husband's reentry from his working environment to the home environment has not been successfully negotiated and is unsettling for both him and his wife.

All of these issues, once clarified, were easily resolved to the satisfaction of both the husband and the wife. This happened in three sessions.

- **Issue #1 Resolution** The husband hung a "punching bag" in their carport. When he needed to release his anger he took 5–10 minutes punching the bag before entering the house. (He loved this! He had had a punching bag as a kid.)
- **Issue #2 Resolution** Once she shared her feeling and felt *heard* by her husband (he was actually very tender), they were able to "brainstorm" about some ways for her to meet people and get involved. Her making friends and having conversations with other adults would meet some of her "togetherness" needs and take some of the pressure off her husband to be the one to provide so much of her relationship needs.
- **Issue #3 Resolution** It was obvious from their initial description that the husband needed some re-entry time before fully engaging with his wife. She was so

very eager to spend time with him that she was not giving him any breathing room when he returned home. I explored with them some ways that they each thought would allow them to have a smooth transition to his reentry. He shared that he would like, after having a brief "hello" kiss, to go into the bedroom and change out of his business suit and then have a chance to read his mail. Once he had about fifteen minutes to do this, he would be ready to spend a nice evening with his wife. She agreed that she would refrain from immediately attempting to engage him. She even suggested that he might want to just sit and watch the six o'clock news before they began to have dinner and spend the evening together. He was delighted with this idea.

When they returned to therapy two weeks later, they reported that the fighting had stopped. They each seemed very pleased with how things were going. No more crying. No more yelling and screaming. No more contemplating divorce. They shared that they were enjoying their evening time together.

All this is to say:

Honor your issues.

Deal with them when they arise.

Don't let them become PROBLEMS!

Zooming out from the couple to the family dynamic, it's important to understand that different cultures encourage different styles of communication and have different rules surrounding it. A young couple composed of a wife of Italian descent, whose family expressed feelings spontaneously and emphatically, and a husband from a conservative English family, who tended to repress and not express feelings, may find themselves frustrated and confused in communicating with each other. Then when the children come along, the children may receive very opposing "rules" about how they should and shouldn't communicate.

This is an issue. It does not have to become a problem.

It has been said that the individuals in every couple are from different cultures. I am sure that there is some truth to this; after all, everyone comes from families with different communication styles and rules. However, the more extreme the differences, the more attention is needed to *understand*, *respect*, *negotiate*, and *accept* one's partner.

A family's communication style and its rules regarding communication are paramount in determining the health of the family and its individual members. That being stated, remember that all communication is learned. Which means that as adults, we each have the power to alter our learned communication style if we so choose. I encourage you to choose to use the healthy communication practices listed below.

Healthy Communication Practices

- **Be Present** Focus on the others in the conversation. Avoid outside distractions.
- **Make Frequent Eye Contact** Making eye contact signals to the other that you are present and that you see them and are interested in the conversation.
- **Listen** Listening goes beyond hearing the words. Listening requires mindfulness. To listen means you are paying attention, not only to the words but to the meaning behind the words. It means being aware of the other's feelings as well as thoughts.
- **Use "I" Messages** This idea has been addressed many times over the years, and yet it remains one of the most difficult practices for people to remember. In my experience, "I" statements make it more likely that the speaker will be heard. The listener is less likely to

begin listening from the place of being *defensive* or *guarded*. (Scenario: a wife speaking to her husband who has arrived home two hours later than he said he would. Wife: "What is wrong with *you*? *You* are so inconsiderate! *You* could have at least called!" Wife using "I" statements: "*I* felt so worried because you were so late. *I* don't understand why you did not call to tell me you were going to be late. *I* am confused and upset.")

- **Share—Be Responsive** If you want to practice healthy communication, it is important to *communicate*! Share and respond to the other. I have seen hundreds of couples in therapy, and a very common complaint from one of the partners is that the other does not respond or share.

- **Deal with Issues Directly and in a Timely Manner** Don't expect others to read your mind. If you have something you want them to know, say it! The longer you carry an issue around inside of you without dealing with it honestly and directly, the more distance is created in the relationship.

- **Take Responsibility** Every healthy communication practice I have listed above requires the participants to take responsibility. Identify and be honest with yourself about your intentions (i.e., do you want to share a concern or admonish the other person? Do you only want to be heard and are not really interested in the other's thoughts and feelings?)

- **Be Collaborative** If you truly desire healthy communication, remember that it is a collaborative endeavor. Working together is paramount.

- **Check Out Your Assumptions and Your Interpretations** I cannot stress this practice enough. Making inaccurate assumptions and responding to your false interpretations of what the other is conveying is a relationship destroyer! CHECK IT OUT!

- **Remember You Are Communicating Verbally and Non-verbally** We do not only communicate with our words but with our tone of voice, our facial expressions, and our body language. Be aware of the messages you are sending verbally and non-verbally, as well as what messages the other is sending.

- **Be Congruent** The more congruent we are with our verbal and non-verbal communication, the less likely we are to send "double messages," which confuse the listener.

- **Be Kind** And as an eighty-eight-year-old friend of mine said recently, "It is simple. BE KIND."

Practices To Foster Healthy Communication

- Set aside time to talk and listen to one another. I encourage families to set aside time for "family meetings." This is so very important for couples to tend to as well.

- Commit to having meals together at least several times a week.

- The old saying "timing is everything" is vitally important when you want or need to have a conversation that may be difficult. It is not a good idea to attempt an important conversation if any of the persons are too tired or busy doing something else.

- It can be enjoyable to have conversations while one or all are engaged in other activities. However, remember that when you or someone is sharing something important, you should minimize distractions. (It's not the best idea to have an important or difficult conversation when you or the other is driving.)

- If you want others to pay attention to you when you are talking, commit to paying attention to them.
- Practice tolerance.

Remember: A healthy and intimate interaction is one in which the participants are fully present with their own thoughts and feelings and are willing to share and listen to one another.

Identifying Communication
Roles and Rules

Here are some questions to help you identify your family's spoken and unspoken rules regarding communication. Think of the following questions in relationship to your family of origin first. Then, if applicable, respond in regard to your current family. How are they similar/different?

1. What was the most effective means of non-verbal communication exhibited by the adults in your family?

2. Did you feel listened to as a child? Did the adults listen more to your *feelings* or *thoughts?* When were you less likely to be listened to? How did you conform to this experience?

3. Was it important for someone in your family to always be right? Do you operate from the position that it is important for you to always be right?

4. What is your belief about confrontation and conflict? Did your parents fight in front of the children? How did that affect you?

5. Do you think of your family as being more spontaneous and open or rigid and closed? Why?

6. How did your family handle problem-solving? Who led the discussion? Who was included? Who got a "vote"?

7. How did your family motivate its members? (With praise or threat of punishment?) How did this style of motivation impact your self-esteem?

8. How did your family use humor? Did this use enhance or distract from having healthy communication?

9. What was the focus of your conversations: Topic-related? Personal? Relational?

10. Did your family handle issues before they became problems? Can you think of a time when a problem could have been avoided if the issue had been dealt with in a timely manner?

11. What is a current issue you are having in your family? Is it avoided or dealt with? Is discussion encouraged or discouraged?

12. Listen to your tone of voice. (Better yet, tape yourself in a discussion and listen to yourself.) Is your voice high or low pitched? Is it pleasant or harsh? Is it loud or soft? What do others tell you about how they experience your delivery of messages? (Especially when you are upset!)

13. Which of the destructive communication practices do you recognize as being prevalent in your family? Which do you frequently use? (Remember awareness is the first step toward change.)

14. Which of the healthy communication practices do you recognize? Which ones are you willing to use more frequently? Do it!

Chapter Four

How Much Togetherness?

The Balance Between Individuality
and Togetherness in a Family

Happiness is having a large, loving, caring,
close-knit family in another city.
GEORGE BURNS

Growing up, my grandmother shared with me one of her
favorite quotes from an unidentified woman, which was,
"There are only two lasting bequests we can hope to give our
children. One of these is roots; the other, wings."

I took this quote to heart. Even before giving birth to my
three sons, I was clear that this was my goal. As a student of
early childhood education, I was introduced to childhood developmental theories and optimal parenting practices. I was clear
as to the importance of providing children with a sense of safety
and security so that they could become healthy, independent,
well-functioning adults. I added to that learning as I continued
in the field of psychology and family therapy.

As John Byng-Hall, a British family therapist, once said,

> [A] parent who can tell stories of having been comforted
> when upset as a child, as well as being supported in order
> to be independent, is likely to have a child who is securely
> attached . . . on the other hand, parents who are full of

grievances about their own parent's unreliable parenting are likely to have insecurely attached children.[1]

Attachment can be thought about as emotional bonds between individuals. These attachment bonds are important as they serve as a survival mechanism, and they endure over time. One's sense of security is highly influenced by the attachment one has to the important persons in one's world, particularly those with whom one is in an intimate relationship.

Byng-Hall's quote speaks to the patterns that travel through the generations in a family system. It is important to note that neurobiologists over the last several decades have established evidence that interpersonal relationships of individuals are at the center of biological survival.

When I was in graduate school, working toward a degree in early childhood education and development (this occurred before working on an advanced degree in counseling psychology), it was apparent to me the immense importance that early relationships play in allowing one to develop or not develop a sense of feeling secure in the world. So, when John Bowlby's work, diving into the importance of attachment for adults as well as infants arrived on the scene, I was delighted. His work on Attachment Theory has been invaluable.[2] Family therapists have long been aware of the importance of an individual's attachment to others and how that influences one's sense of self and of being in the world.

It is now understood that the process of attachment is strongly tied to biology, particularly neurophysiology. Daniel Siegel is a contemporary psychiatrist and writer who specializes in interpersonal neurobiology. Siegel espouses that the body performs as a collective intelligence using interpersonal processes, which revolve around dialogues that are scripted in the neurophysiology of experience, emotion, meaning, memory, and action.[3]

I believe this process begins even before one is born. After all, we are created *attached* in the womb to our birth mothers.

Attachment is not only experienced physically but also emotionally. It is through children's experiences in their families that they learn if others are or are not trustworthy and available to support their emotional needs. They learn whether or not it is safe to be vulnerable. As we grow into adulthood, we turn these experiences into beliefs about relationships. These beliefs color what we expect in a relationship with our significant others and with our children. There is a direct correlation between feeling secure as a child and becoming an independent adult who is capable of forming secure attachment bonds with significant others. One's sense of self-worth and identity absolutely influence one's capacity to attain a sense of independence and individuality while maintaining connectedness to others.

Some families foster individuality and separateness, while others demand togetherness. The degree of family closeness or separateness depends not only on the family pattern but also on the developmental needs of the family. There is a need for families with young children to be more connected. As the children mature, the family will hopefully encourage their children to become more separate, thus supporting individuality and independence. In a healthy family this process occurs simultaneously, as the individuals also experience a healthy interdependence on one another.

Neither closeness nor separateness is inherently good or bad. It is the degree and the impact on the individuals in the family that indicates healthy versus unhealthy. For example, I have friends whose adult children call them every day. This practice seems to benefit both the parent and the child. They both seem to enjoy this daily contact. However, for others, this closeness would not be experienced so positively. One or both of the parties might feel burdened or resentful of the daily expectation of taking the time to have yet another conversation. It is not one size fits all. What works for the individual members in one family does not necessarily work for the individuals in another family.

In the example above, I refer to only the two individuals involved in the phone calling. If they are not the only two members of the family, then it follows that other family members could be impacted by the daily phone call. The adult child's partner may resent the time his wife spends on the phone with her mother. The adult child's sister may be jealous, or relieved, that another daughter is so "close" to their mother.

When two or more persons in the family share a "closeness" in which others do not, tension may be created within the system as a whole. A parent may be jealous or hurt that one of the children has a closer relationship with the other parent. This dynamic occurs in intact families as well as blended families. It is more common than not that a stepparent feels "left out." In a situation where a child bonds with a stepparent, the original parent may experience jealousy or delight, or both. If the child moves closer to the stepparent than he is to the original parent, the original parent may become emotionally distraught and confused, or immensely relieved. Obviously, the responses to this scenario vary. Not only do responses differ between individuals, responses can also vary within an individual given the circumstances, age, and their stage of development. Closeness and distance are ever-present conditions we need to negotiate.

Togetherness and the Developmental Life Cycle

The question of "how much togetherness?" begins to present itself about the time a child turns two years old. For some children, beginning to walk is when they begin the process of individuation, i.e., experiencing one's self as a separate person. They want to wander off and explore the world by themselves, as long as they can look back and see the parent nearby. Those children will run back to get a pat, a kiss, or just to "touch base." Other children will only move a few feet away, wanting and needing the parent to be at arm's length at all times. There is not a right or wrong here; every individual has their own wants, needs, and appropriate time to begin the process of individuation.

If there is a problem at this point of development, it is more likely to show up with the parent. Can the parent tolerate the child running halfway across the yard to try to catch the bird? Does the parent immediately leap up and follow, or call the child back? Or does the parent resent the child who won't move more than a few feet away?

Fast forward to the teenage years. This is the time in the developmental life cycle of the family when we often see the greatest struggle with the issue of autonomy and individuation. Most parents are somewhat prepared for what is believed to be the inevitable power struggle between the teenager who wants more freedom and the parents who think the child is not yet mature enough to handle more freedom. Parents who have established a clear hierarchy and have set appropriate rules given the developmental life cycle of a child are more likely to traverse this often rocky terrain of raising a teenager with more ease than those who have not. If the family is open and flexible, the road to transitioning from having a child who becomes a teenager to one who is heading for young adulthood is a smoother one.

The family then moves to the stage of "launching" the young adult. It has been my observation that in the last decade, this has become a more difficult time in the life cycle of the family. Statistics have shown that more and more young adults continue living at home once they have graduated from high school or college. The reason for this is often financial. A commonly held value is that an adult child needs to find employment and begin to live more independently; currently, however, this is often difficult for many young adults because their incomes do not match the high costs of living.

There are situations in which the child is living at home for reasons other than financial ones. One possibility is that the child, who is now an adult child, does not feel self-assured in a way that would allow him to become individuated and independent. Another possibility is that one or more of the parents are reluctant to truly "launch" the child. When this is the case, it is usually more unconscious than conscious within the parent.

There are situations in which an adult child chooses to live with a parent or parents, and this circumstance is not a failure of launching. This can, indeed, be a healthy functioning option for the individual family members. The key is that this arrangement is mutually beneficial to the family members and that none of the individuals are sacrificing their own wants and needs.

Togetherness and Extended Family

Also important within the question of togetherness is the issue of how much time a family is going to spend with their extended family, i.e., "the in-laws." Is having dinner every Sunday night at Mom's experienced as positive, neutral, or negative to any of the family members involved?

I remember my immediate family of my father, mother, brother, sister, and myself gathering at my grandmother's (father's mother) along with my aunt, uncle, and three cousins every Sunday night in the summer for a cookout. This occurred from the time I was a small child until I graduated from high school. I always looked forward to it. It was a fun and joyful time for me, for us to all be together. I do not remember ever hearing either my father or mother or siblings complain.

When I became a family therapist, I quickly learned that not everyone experienced these Sunday gatherings in the same positive way as I did. I heard the expectation to attend a family gathering referred to as a "command performance." I learned that one or more of the individuals in the family felt resentful that there was a requirement that one must attend the gathering.

The aforementioned scenario is not unusual. There is one surprising case I remember involving a woman in her sixties whose husband had recently passed away. She expressed resentment that her children expected her to purchase and prepare all the food every Sunday evening for a family meal. This was the first time I had heard the mother/grandmother express resentment regarding this family tradition. I had, heretofore, only heard the resentment expressed by an adult child or grandchild regarding the expectation that they must attend such gatherings.

Whenever clients express any kind of negative feeling regarding togetherness, my goal is to help them understand what is behind their feelings and to explore options for the possibility of their experiencing a different internal feeling. This often requires an individual to rewrite the story they are telling themselves. For example, if I am sitting with a teenager who is complaining about how "boring" it is to go to his grandparents' every Friday evening, I would encourage him to explore a response other than "boring." I might begin by asking him about a time when he did not experience boredom when going to the Friday night gathering. Is there anything from that story that can be used to create a current, more positive story? Or is there anything in that story that can inspire him to be creative in how he might be present at the family gathering and not be bored? What would he like to feel when he is there? How can he promote those feelings?

Once we have explored the individual's internal responses, I then encourage them to explore possible conversations with others involved, and their own behavioral changes that could be helpful in dealing with the "togetherness" issues in their relationships.

There is no doubt that separateness and togetherness in families has been and is influenced by the broader society. When we were a largely rural society, family members usually lived nearer one another. In our modern world, family members often live many miles apart. Modern technology has certainly helped us to stay connected. I am so grateful that I can FaceTime with my grandchildren who live in different states. I remember when my oldest grandchild was about fourteen months old, and we were visiting on Skype shortly after we had had an in-person visit. He attempted to crawl into the screen so I could hold him. I was both deeply touched and mortified at the same time. There is nothing that can truly replicate face-to-face interaction. Hearing and seeing is good; however, not being able to smell or physically touch is a loss.

Modern technology may help us stay connected, but it can also foster dis-connection and loss of intimacy. The use of cell phones, iPads, laptops, and other devices creates distance, even when the user is unaware that it's happening.

Several years ago, I was seeing a couple, both in their forties. When they shared with me that their main form of communication in the week before our session was texting while together in their home, I was aghast. It was clear to me that I needed them to each explore how committed they each were to creating better communication and intimacy.

Autonomy and Individuation

Autonomy, individuation, and separation from one's family of origin is an ongoing process within each individual. I have seen seventy-year-olds who are still operating with messages and beliefs they received as children that are inhibiting them from being their true selves.

For example, I saw a seventy-two-year-old woman who had recently lost her husband. She came into therapy seeking support as she was in the process of grieving. After we had worked together for a while, she shared with me that she had always wanted to go to France. Her husband had no interest in traveling outside the United States, so she put her desire on the back burner. As we began talking about how she wanted to create the next phase of her life, she began exploring the possibility of making a trip to France. She had a female friend who was encouraging my client to join her on a trip to Paris.

My client identified that she was experiencing a great deal of anxiety. As we explored her anxious feelings, she recalled a message that she had received from her father when she was but a young girl. Her father was in WWII and was among the American troops that were part of the Normandy invasion, along the coast of France. Her father was traumatized by this experience. He was vocal about "never" wanting to set foot on French soil again. My client had taken her father's fear and his message to heart.

Our work together focused on helping her to discover and claim her own beliefs. She was able to separate her beliefs from those she held within her that belonged to her father. Her anxiety dissipated, and she went on the trip with her friend to Paris. She reported having enjoyed the trip immensely and was planning on taking more trips out of the country.

Of all the issues presented in couple and family therapy, the question of "how much togetherness?" is one that stays near the top of the list.

When an individual becomes a part of a couple, each individual brings with them his or her own issues of separateness and togetherness in dealing with how much they can each tolerate being connected to each other and their own and their partner's family of origin. How much separateness and togetherness they each feel comfortable with within their relationship is dependent upon the degree to which they have successfully achieved autonomy and independence from their families' emotional systems.

Murray Bowen, whom I mentioned earlier, was one of the founders of Family Systems Theory. One of the many major contributions Bowen gave to the field was the idea of the *differentiation of self.* He defined *differentiation* as one's ability to separate their own emotional and intellectual functioning from their family's, thus achieving independence and maturity without losing the capacity of emotional connection. He postulated that more differentiated individuals are much more secure about their identity and thus are less likely to sacrifice their own wants and needs in exchange for love and acceptance.[4]

If an adult has not successfully *differentiated*, then that individual cannot be free to be and feel who she truly is. In other words, she will not be able to be in a true relationship with herself! One must be able to be connected to one's self to disconnect from the emotional reactivity in one's family.

By disconnecting from one's family's emotional reactivity, one is then free to CHOOSE not only how to react but what to feel.

Emotional Reactivity

When we are no longer able to change a situation,
we are challenged to change ourselves.

Everything can be taken from a man but one thing: the
last of the human freedoms—to choose one's attitude in any
given set of circumstances, to choose one's own way.

Between stimulus and response there is a space. In
that space is our power to choose our response. In our
response lies our growth and our freedom.

ATTRIBUTED TO VIKTOR FRANKL[5]

Bowen considered the family as an emotional system that includes the present members who live in the household as well as the extended family, both living and deceased. He believed that all the members—present and absent, living or dead—make up the emotional system. He also believed that the emotional systems of previous generations of the family are present in the current family. He referred to this as the *nuclear family emotional system.*

Every family attempts to find its level of comfort in allowing for each person to individuate versus being together both physically and psychologically. Togetherness becomes problematic when the individuals experience being "stuck together" in an unhealthy way. Bowen calls this *fusion* or *enmeshment.* Fusion is the blending of oneself with another in such a way that there is a profound loss of self.

As humans, we have an inherent need for togetherness. The struggle to become an autonomous individual and the concurrent drive toward togetherness contributes to stress, tension, and anxiety in the individual and in the family unit. This struggle between individuality and togetherness is ongoing. We are constantly adjusting and readjusting.

What degree of intimacy do we long for?

How much closeness do we want?

How much connection or lack thereof can we tolerate?

What is our level of need for approval?

As I mentioned previously, Bowen's differentiation of self involves an individual's ability to distinguish between their own feelings and thoughts while in relationship with others. The individual's emotional reactivity is a key factor here. Of course, feelings and emotions are desirable in relationships. How can there *be* a relationship without them? But while this is true, it is emotions and feeling that generate the most distress in relationships.

How an individual reacts and responds emotionally is key to the degree of differentiation one attains. If a person understands she can choose how to react to a feeling, and not be driven by the emotion itself, then she is less likely to be controlled by her emotions. She experiences a lesser degree of emotional reactivity. She, therefore, is her own executor. She relates to others from a place of personal power. She calms her emotional reaction by using her thinking to decide how to respond—as opposed to instantaneously *reacting*.

As humans, we have both feelings and thinking capabilities. Learning to delineate, i.e., differentiate, between the two is essential in becoming a fully actualized person, an individual who is confident in truly being themselves. A healthy, differentiated person chooses to step back, takes stock of the situation, and recognizes and owns their feelings, but does not automatically *react*. They make a conscious decision about what they want, how they feel, and how they *choose to respond* in the situation. The focus here is on SELF and one's emotional responses; it is not dependent on the other. The other may agree, or not. The other may understand, or not. The other may decide to behave differently, or not. We must relinquish the idea that it is our job to get the other to agree, understand, or change their behavior and that we need the other to do so for us to be all right.

The healthy, differentiated person knows how to calm down emotional reactivity AND stay in relationship with the other person(s). (Unless it is unsafe to do so. If there is emotional or physical abuse, it is not wise to choose to stay connected in a way that puts one in peril. There are relationships that are toxic. Choosing to disengage is often the healthiest option an individual can make.)

Staying emotionally present in an ongoing relationship when one is emotionally upset can be difficult. Sometimes an individual has to distance to calm down. If a person stays distant for too long, however, the relationship could be jeopardized. Staying distant can result in being cut off from having an emotional relationship.

People distance in all kinds of ways. Lack of communication, substance abuse, affairs, and workaholism are some of the common ways people create distance to reduce the anxiety they experience in a relationship. Being too distant can be as dysfunctional as being too close. In both couples and families, the balance of how much togetherness is too little or too much shifts regularly, depending on many factors.

Too Close

When a family is experiencing a high degree of stress, for instance, it may tend to gravitate toward togetherness to help relieve the anxiety that often accompanies change. This togetherness can be comforting and offer support that is needed for the individual members of the family. However, if this togetherness persists and develops into fusion or enmeshment, then there may be one or more of the individuals in the family system that may be negatively affected. Fusion occurs when family members merge their intellectual and emotional selves.

A twenty-three-year-old young woman came into therapy. She shared that she was extremely depressed and unmotivated. When taking the family history, I learned that she had returned home two years earlier. At that time, she was in her second year of college and had decided to come home to be with her family while her mother was dying of cancer. Her mother died six months later. The family grieved together. Her older brother, her only sibling, returned to his out-of-state graduate program a month after the death of their mother. The young woman, however, stayed at home with her father, who returned to his job. Her focus became to take care of her father. She functioned as a homemaker, doing tasks her mother had done. Over the course of the next two years, she became depressed.

I initially diagnosed her to be suffering from unresolved grief. However, after a while, I felt like I was "missing" something. I invited the father into a session. As I listened to their discussion, I realized that he was sending her mixed messages. His overt message was, "go back to college and get on with your life as a young woman." But his covert message, which was totally out of his awareness, was, "I miss your mother so much and cannot bear to be alone."

This family's coming together for support during the last days of the mother's life and at the time of her death was timely and positive. The daughter, out of love, empathy, and devotion to her father, became sacrificial, which was detrimental to her emotional and mental health. Her father was unaware that his daughter's choosing to stay home with him was causing her to lose herself and her own dreams for her future.

I was able to support both the father in his grief and the daughter in her grief and to help them disengage from the enmeshment that had developed. The daughter returned to college. I continued to work with the father, supporting him to create a new life for himself while honoring his love for his wife. As often occurs in this situation, individuals may have trouble moving on after a loss because they mistakenly believe it diminishes the love they had for the person for whom they are grieving. Grief therapy helps guide and support individuals through the grieving process.

In an enmeshed family, the members are over-involved and extremely dependent on one another. If an individual attempts to separate, the others may experience increased anxiety. Children are often seen as extensions of the adults. Everyone takes everything personally. If a child does something wrong or makes a mistake, the parents see it as a reflection on them. Parents become overly focused on their children's behavior and how it reflects on them in the community.

Enmeshed families are over-protective, even smothering. Everyone must share the same opinion or the family feels threatened. The child who is in an enmeshed family system will more likely find it difficult to develop a clear sense of self. This child may find it difficult to separate her thoughts and feelings from those of her parents. She is likely to experience a high degree of stress because her family dictates her emotions. She does not regard her own inner experience. She thinks what she has been told to think, feels what she has been assigned to feel. She may become overly dependent when in relationship with others. She will most likely lack self-confidence and self-reliance. If she rebels, another family member (usually a parent) may become depressed or anxious. Often this parent(s) will "choose" another child or individual on which to focus.

Too Distant

In some families, there is too much distance. These are families in which everyone is pretty much on their own. The members are lonely. They do not share time, thoughts, or feelings. They look outside the family to connect with others.

If a child has a parent or two parents who are both under-involved, he will likely feel insecure, lonely, and have low self-esteem. Often his parents are experiencing similar emotions. It is possible, although rare, that this child may individuate very quickly and learn to listen to his inner voice. He may, however, have difficulty in forming deep and healthy connections with others later in his life. He may fear intimacy and choose relationships that are shallow and superficial.

A healthy developmental path allows for the child to grow up into an emotionally separate person. A person who can have their own thoughts and experience their own feelings and yet remain emotionally connected to their family. They can claim their own thoughts. The healthy differentiated person can relate to others openly and honestly, taking full responsibility for their feelings, thoughts, and behaviors.

This balance between individuation and "stuck-togetherness" depends largely on how well the parents themselves have been able to individuate while maintaining an emotional connection to their own families. Some persons find the only way they can get separate is by distancing from their family of origin. They may distance temporarily or permanently, thus cutting off from the family or a particular family member.

A physical *cutoff* occurs when at least one family member chooses not to engage in any current, observable interactions. The cutoff may be physical or emotional. Emotional cutoffs are more difficult to manage; a person can live two thousand miles away and have avoided contact for decades and still be emotionally responding to family. Cutting off physically can be a way individuals deceive themselves that they are free of their family. However, as the saying goes, "Wherever I go, there I am." Even when one stops contact with family members, one is still carrying them in one's psyche. We deceive ourselves into believing that we are truly emancipated.

Bowen proposed the idea of the multigenerational transmission process, in which one generation can transmit an emotional process to the next generation. Bowen believed that cutoffs in a family get repeated from generation to generation unless the unresolved conflict is addressed. In an ongoing relationship, the pattern of cutting off is a temporary fix. It is not a solution to the anxiety produced by extremely intense emotions.

As a young family therapist, I thought I should help an individual who had cut off from his or her family to reconnect. Although I still believe that this is optimal in many cases, I know that there are times when retaining the distance or cutoff is the healthy choice. There are relationships that are too toxic or detrimental physically or emotionally, in which a cutoff is necessary for self-preservation and healing. It is my job as the therapist to help the client move from a place of reactivity to one of choice, a place free from emotional reactivity (not easy to attain, but an immensely worthwhile endeavor).

Freeing oneself from emotional reactivity does not dictate that you cannot feel empathy. This truth is often confusing. For some persons, disconnecting from feeling empathy is a part of their individuation process. These individuals believe that caring about someone and being concerned for them means that they then need to "take care of" the person or situation. As one successfully engages in the process of individuation, it is important to shift this false belief.

In working with many families who have a family member who is addicted to drugs or alcohol, I have often experienced the issue of destructive versus healthy empathy. Because these family members care and are concerned about their addicted family member, they tend to stay in "rescue" mode, which is an example of destructive empathy. When their many attempts at "rescuing" have failed, they tend to gravitate toward either "giving up" or trying harder to rescue. For many, "giving up" not only means giving up their unsuccessful attempts at rescuing but giving up having their feelings about the addict and for the situation. Over time, my hope for them is that they can stop attempting to rescue and have healthy empathy for both themselves and their addicted family member.

The Balance Between Togetherness and Separateness

Humans need relationships to survive. We enter this world dependent on others for our mere survival. We need others for both physical and emotional nurturing. Our early connections are key to our connecting in future relationships. We need relationship "togetherness" not only to survive but also to thrive. Individuals need connection. There is a strong correlation between one's physical and emotional health and the health of the relationships we experience throughout our lives. As Robert Waldinger said in his 2016 TED Talk about the Harvard Study of Adult Development,

> [I]t wasn't their middle-age cholesterol levels that pre-
> dicted how they were going to grow old . . . It was how
> satisfied they were in their relationships. The people
> who were most satisfied with their relationships at age
> fifty were healthiest at age eighty.[6]

As stated previously, a healthy developmental path allows for the child to grow up becoming an emotionally separate person—a person who can have their own thoughts and experience their own feelings and remain emotionally connected to their family.

As a person becomes a more individuated adult, the task then becomes how much togetherness, with whom, and how frequently?

How Much Separateness and Togetherness?

Growing Up in Your Family

1. Did the family you grew up in eat meals together? Did that feel good to you? What would you have liked to have been different?

2. Did your family talk with one another while eating or driving in the car? Did you feel comfortable or uncomfortable? Why? What would you have liked to have been different?

For these next questions, rate your family of origin using a scale from 1–10. Use 1 to signify almost always separate (distant). Use 10 to signify almost always together (closeness). There are no wrong answers. This is to help you evaluate your past experiences and to evaluate what changes you might desire. (Think of descriptive words regarding your observations and experiences in your family. Did you experience warmth, caring, emotional distance, physical distance, being smothered, coldness, disdain, conflict, love?)

3. Where would you rate your parents' relationship in terms of separateness and togetherness? Have your relationships with significant others been similar or different?

4. What was your mother's level of separateness and togetherness with her parents? What is your level with your mother? With this set of grandparents?

5. What was your father's level of separateness and togetherness with his parents? What is your level with your father? With this set of grandparents?

6. If you had siblings, rate the level of separateness and closeness with each. How has that changed over time?

7. Where on the scale would you put the overall experience you had growing up in your family regarding separateness and togetherness? Did that level of separateness and togetherness feel good to you?

Reflecting on Your Current Status

1. How would you scale your current level of separateness and togetherness regarding the actual time you spend together physically with members of your family of origin? Does that feel satisfactory to you?

2. How would you scale your current level of separateness and togetherness regarding your emotional connection to the members of your family of origin? Does that feel satisfactory to you?

3. How have the past experiences of separateness (distance) and togetherness (closeness) influenced your current relationships?

4. Have you attempted to repeat your family's patterns of separateness and togetherness, or have you intentionally tried to do it differently?

5. Do you think you give your children more or less autonomy and freedom than you experienced in your family?

6. Do you believe that your relationship patterns with your family are impacting your friendships or other relationships?

Knowing these patterns of relatedness can help you decide to be more flexible and constructive about the kind of relationships you want for yourself—and if you have children or relate frequently with members of a younger generation, the legacy of relating that you desire to model for them.

Chapter Five

Why a Three-Legged Stool?

Family Triangles

When the wind blows wrong, I can hear it today.
Then my mother's worry stops all play

And, as if in its rightful place,
My father's frown divides my face.
NAOMI REPLANSKY, "AN INHERITANCE"

If you think of a stool with only two legs, you can imagine the difficulty one would have maintaining balance. By adding a third leg, creating a tripod or triangle, the stool becomes stabilized. In a family, a triad is the smallest stable grouping. Families have developmental stressors and situational stressors as a matter of course. Therefore, triangular alignments are expected to arise in the system's structure. Their function is to attempt to balance the family system. This is neither good nor bad.

One of the patterns of interaction that most family therapists address is that of triangulation. Murray Bowen and other systems theorists maintain that whenever a twosome's relationship becomes too close or too distant, creating anxiety in one or more persons in the dyad, there is a tendency to triangle a third person or thing into the relationship to reduce the anxiety and to attempt to stabilize the family system.[1]

A healthy family system promotes the growth and development of the individuals involved. Thus, the healthy family system *serves* the individuals. In an unhealthy system, an individual serves the system instead, to the degree that this service becomes harmful to the growth and development of the individual. So, a triangle is harmful if one or more of the persons in the triangle are denied the safety, security, and freedom to grow and develop personally and relationally.

Triangles may be either functional or dysfunctional. Functional triangles are generally short-lived and help the family stabilize. Generally, they consist of one or more persons holding a different role in the family for a defined amount of time.

When I gave birth to my third son, my mother-in-law came and stayed for a week to help. My mother-in-law took over cooking and caring for the other two children, as well as helping me with the baby. I was dependent on her to be my "stand-in" during this developmental, life-transition stage. She did the "mothering." I suffered from pneumonia at the time of my baby's birth and therefore required some mothering myself. Almost all my contact with the other members of my family and friends, except for my baby and my spouse, was through my mother-in-law. My triangulating her in my relationships was temporary until I could regain my strength. Her help stabilized my relationship with my spouse, my other sons, my new infant, and my friends and neighbors.

Typically, family systems theorists tend to refer to triangulation as a "red flag." That is because most of the time triangles stabilizing a dyad are unhealthy. They are unhealthy because one or both members of the dyad use the third person or thing to divert attention away from the relationship rather than resolving the relationship issues that exist between the two of them. Thus, the dyad's relationship issues are not resolved, and the person being triangulated, particularly if this person is a child, may suffer emotional and mental harm.

Triangles with Children

If the dyad is a couple who have children, the children become the obvious target for triangulation. One or more children may be brought into a triangle to blur marital conflict or to make parenting issues the place where the marital conflict is expressed.

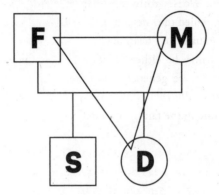

5.1. Parent/child triangle

There are some common themes around triangulation with children, which I have thought about many times over the many years that I have been working with families.

The three most common themes I have experienced are:

1. Child as Comforter (Peacemaker, Rescuer),
2. Child as Parent (Parentified Child), and
3. Child as Focus of Attention (Child with Behavioral Problems, or the Sick Child—emotionally, mentally, and/or physically).

I will give some examples of these themes.

Child as Comforter (Peacemaker, Rescuer)

A client of mine, Ruth, would come into a session after visiting her mother (M) and stepfather (SF) and would describe herself as feeling anxious and depressed. She was baffled as to how the *same* dynamic always seemed to unfold whenever she would visit them. Every scenario was different. But the dynamics remained the same.

Scene #1 (Morning. All three at the breakfast table.)

M to SF: "Would you get me another cup of coffee?"

SF (reading newspaper): "As soon as I finish this article."

M: "Oh for heaven's sake!"

SF: "Get it yourself. I'm not your servant!"

(Ruth feels distress. She wants to de-stress the situation. So she enters into the triangle and attempts to rescue them from another disagreement.)

Ruth: "It's O.K. I'll get you some coffee, Mother."

M: "Don't take him off the hook! He never wants to do anything I ask. I think you like him better than you like me!"

(Mother stomps out of the room. Ruth feels sick. All she wanted to do was HELP!)

How many times have you heard yourself or someone else saying these words, "all I was trying to do was to *help*" and being mystified as to why you ended up feeling *bad* when all you were trying to do was help?

Scene #2 (Mother and Ruth leaving to go to the mall. Stepfather planning to prepare dinner to have for them when they return.)

As they exit, out of Ruth's earshot, SF asks M:

SF: "Will you stop by the vegetable stand and get some fresh tomatoes for our salad?"

M: "Sure. We will be back by six."

(5:45 PM: Gals return to house without the tomatoes.)

SF: "Where are the tomatoes?"

M: "Oh, I forgot. We can have the salad without the tomatoes."

SF: "I have spent the last hour preparing food for all of us and you couldn't even get tomatoes!"

(He throws down the dishtowel and turns his back to them.)

Ruth (to the rescue): "I'll run out and get the tomatoes."

(She gets the tomatoes. The family dinner is strained. Mother and stepfather are not speaking. Ruth tries to carry on a conversation and feels anxious once again.)

This same pattern repeats over and over again. How did Ruth get into this pattern of Comforter/Rescuer? It is most likely that one or both of her parents set her up to be triangulated in their disputes, and she obliged by attempting to be the rescuer. She accepted the role of Peacemaker as a child. The Peacemaker often takes on the task of rescuing.

In therapy, we explored Ruth's anxious feelings and realized they were connected to her futile efforts to reduce the tension between her parents. She also became aware that she repeats the role of being the Peacemaker and Rescuer in settings other than her parents' home.

Once she was aware of her part in accepting the role as Peacemaker and Rescuer, she realized she could choose to continue in the role or abdicate! Of course, if she decides to get out of those roles, it will be important for her to give up feeling responsible for her parents' relationship. She would, hopefully, learn to soothe herself when she experienced the strain between them and understand that she did not have to "fix" them before she could be separate from their feelings.

As an adult, Ruth entered the triangle willingly. She was, however, well entrenched in this pattern since childhood. It is usually an adult who engages a child in a triangle. Once snared, it can be very difficult to get free. It takes awareness, willingness to make a new decision, and the courage to take action in order to succeed in escaping the hold of a familial triangle.

It is not unusual for children to be triangulated by parents who want the child to be in the role of the Peacemaker (Rescuer) as we have just witnessed. Triangles are inevitable. That one is in a triangle is not so much the issue; it is how one manages (thinks, feels, and acts) from that position. When triangles are recognized, then some choices can be made. You can decide whether or not to stay in the triangle, and if you do decide to stay, you can choose how you want to exist in it.

If you choose to stay in the triangle, it is important to remain aware of the dynamics, have open communication, and to not take on the anxiety of the other two in the triangle. No easy task!

Awareness is the first step to discontinuing engagement in an unhealthy pattern of thoughts and actions. Communicating your intentions to disengage in a triangle can be accomplished by having a discussion with the others involved or by changing your behavior. Depending on the emotional and mental health of the others involved, it may serve you better to not engage in a conversation that you are sure will end up in chaos and disaster.

My client, Carol, complained during one of her sessions that every time her sister and brother-in-law got into a fight, he would call Carol and ask her to "try and talk some sense" into her sister (his wife). Carol would call her sister and attempt to calm her down. Carol felt in the role of "referee." She claimed that she did not want to be referee anymore. She told her brother-in-law that she did not want him to call her when he and her sister got into an argument. He stopped asking her to talk to her sister but continued calling to complain. Carol told him that she understood his frustration, but that she not only did not want to get in the middle of their arguments, she did not want to hear his complaints about her sister. She recommended couple therapy for the umpteenth time. The next time he called to complain she told him, "I know you are upset, but I am not available to discuss this with you." It took her about three times of setting this clear boundary for him to get that she meant business. Carol had successfully freed herself from this family triangle.

My client Kirk, aged 23, entered therapy because he was in an unhealthy triangle with his parents. One or both were often calling him to "rescue" them from whatever was the most recent dilemma. His parents were both in their late fifties; his mother had a diagnosis of bipolar and was taking medication, while his father used alcohol as a coping strategy. Kirk had tried to talk with them about their pattern of wanting him to be their rescuer, but they would chastise him and tell him he was a terrible son. He learned that it was not in his best interest to attempt to have a dialogue with them, and decided that "actions speak louder than words."

Kirk gave himself permission to give up attempting to rescue them and took actions to take care of himself. For example, he decided not to answer the phone immediately when either one called. He would listen to the message, and if it did not involve his being asked to rescue one of them, he would call them back. If they needed something, he would text them to say he was busy, or suggest someone else for them to call. So if his mother called to say, "The faucet is leaking and your father won't fix it!" he would either not respond or would send a text saying, "Call a plumber."

Child as Parent (Parentified Child)

Children are also pulled into triangles by a parent to occupy a parental role. This child becomes the Parentified Child (as I did for a short time while my father was in the hospital, which I discussed in chapter 2).

A child who gets *stuck* in this role is likely to become anxious and/or depressed and possibly insecure. This is often seen in families in which one of the parents is a substance abuser. It is also commonly seen in a family with a single parent. In chapter 2, the importance of the parental hierarchy was addressed, and I gave some personal examples of a child being in a parental role. As I stated in that chapter, there are times a child takes on a parental role that helps the family system and does not harm the child.

As the oldest child, I often felt that I was placed in the parent role by both of my parents. My mother expected me to help with the chores in ways that were way beyond my level of maturity. When I was four years old, my baby sister was born. My sweet baby sister came home from the hospital with infected fingernails and toenails. My younger brother (age 2) and I both had the mumps. My poor mother would come into the bedroom to care for my brother and me. She would then step out of our room, drop all of her clothes to the floor, and bathe before entering the baby's room so that she could treat the baby's infected nails and care for the baby.

After several weeks of this, when we children were all well, my mother had what was called back in those days a nervous breakdown. She was suffering a mental health emergency rather than a diagnosable condition, but it was frightening to her and to us. She was completely exhausted under the intense stress and could no longer cope with functioning under this physical and emotional duress. My memory is fuzzy, but it seemed like this condition lasted for several weeks.

I remember standing on a stool at the kitchen sink washing and drying dishes while my father put the little ones to bed. I was four! At the time, I just thought I was doing what big girls do.

As a Parentified Child, I did indeed feel special. But lurking beneath the surface of my feeling special was uneasiness. I knew, as most parentified children do, that something was NOT RIGHT. And it did not feel good!

When a child is drawn into a triangle where they're assigned a parental role, the child may become sacrificial. A child or individual becomes sacrificial when they give up "too much" of SELF (child's own wants, needs, and dreams) to take on the role of the Parentified Child. This is harmful! This is more likely to happen when a child is *stuck* in a parental role for an extended period of time.

It is not uncommon for a child to become the Parentified Child in single parent families. This situation is often born out of logistical needs. The following example, however, includes an intact family of a mother, father, daughter (older child), and son.

The mother worked days, while the father worked a night shift in a local factory. Before the mother returned home and after the father left for work, there was a period of two to three hours that coincided with the son and daughter coming home after school. The daughter had to help her brother with his homework, as well as doing her own. She was required to fix the evening meal so that it would be ready when her mother returned from a hard day's work. She would also clean up the kitchen after dinner. This went on day after day, year after year.

When this daughter came into therapy after graduating from nursing school, she was severely depressed. As we worked together, it became evident that she had never had time or permission to acknowledge and tend to her own wants and needs. There is no blame here; the parents were not intentionally setting their daughter up to feel depressed. They needed her to step into the parental role to keep the family functioning. However, my client got so stuck in this role that she relinquished herself to it. As we worked together, she gave herself permission to be aware of her feelings, her wants and needs, and her dreams. She began practicing self-care. In so doing, her depression lifted.

My hope is that in families in which one or more of the children are needed to step into parental roles, the family will find a way to foster their children's freedom to be children. I know of many families who have been able to do so. It takes awareness and intention on the part of the parent(s) to make sure this happens.

The example above describes a child who has been parentified because of the needs of the family to function given the circumstances. There are also situations when parents pull a child into a parental position to mitigate their own anxiety, depression, insecurities, or loneliness.

This brings to mind a family who came for therapy. The mother brought in her thirteen-year-old daughter, who was exhibiting depression and self-harm. The daughter had been observed by a teacher repeatedly jabbing her arm with a pencil. The daughter shared that it was really upsetting to her that her mother would treat her as a confidant and ask her for advice regarding the relationships the mother had with different men she was dating—including the sexual aspects of these relationships. The mother was not observing healthy boundaries with her daughter, and was placing the child in a parental role of parenting her. This had to STOP. Fortunately, the mother was open to hearing her daughter; it was obvious to me that the mother would not have come with her daughter to therapy if she did not care. I worked with them on creating clear boundaries, and then referred the mother for individual therapy. She clearly needed and wanted someone to talk to!

Child as Focus of Attention (Child with Behavioral Problems, or the Sick Child)

Children may also be triangulated by being cast in the role of Child as Focus of Attention. In this role, the child helps to reduce the tension between the parents or distracts a parent from his own internal mental or emotional stress by acting out and getting into trouble. This allows the parents to focus on the child rather than themselves, each other, or the relationship. Some parents use more than one child to fill this role. They may even rotate through the children, triangulating them in this and other roles.

Another unfortunately common role that children take on or are assigned in order to help reduce the anxiety in one or both parents is that of the Sick Child. Dealing with the Sick Child is another way parents divert relational and intrapsychic stress. The child gets physically, emotionally, or mentally ill. It is important to note that this is not within the awareness of the parents and the child. This is happening on the unconscious level, not the conscious. The parents are not consciously making the child sick. The child is not consciously choosing to be sick.

School phobia is an example. Mr. Clark brought in his eight-year-old son, Tommy, because Tommy refused to go to school. He had been diagnosed with school phobia—fear of going to school. Every morning when Mr. Clark attempted to take Tommy to school, Tommy would scream and cry. He would kick his father and then fall onto the floor wailing. Mr. Clark had tried physically putting Tommy into the car and driving him to school. Tommy was relentless in his continuing to yell and cry. On several occasions, Mr. Clark left Tommy at school at the instruction of the principal and teacher. Each time, within several hours, the school would call telling Mr. Clark that Tommy was inconsolable and was disrupting the class. They would ask Mr. Clark to come and take Tommy home.

As I took a family history, it became apparent that Tommy had stopped going to school shortly after his mother moved out of the house to live with her lover. Mr. Clark worked from his home.

I scheduled an individual session with Mr. Clark. He shared with me that he was severely depressed and had even thought about suicide. I suggested we meet several more times without Tommy, as I suspected that Tommy was school phobic because he could sense his father's anguish and felt he needed to stay home from school to "watch over him." I coached Mr. Clark on how to reassure his son that he was going to be all right.

I helped Mr. Clark process his grief regarding the ending of his marriage. He decided to continue with me individually while the two of them periodically came in together. I helped Mr. Clark learn to parent his son as the boy grieved the impending divorce and the loss of his mother being in the same house. As Mr. Clark began his healing, Tommy started attending school. His attendance was sporadic at first but within a brief time was regular.

In this case, school phobia was an accurate diagnosis. The question was which treatment modality would best address this problem. The choices were individual therapy for Tommy or family therapy, which would address issues in the family system. I framed Tommy's problem as a symptom of stress in the family system. The problem did not reside in Tommy; it resided in the family system.

This kind of situation is not unusual. That being said, it is important to acknowledge that some children are biologically, emotionally, or mentally ill and that these illnesses do not develop in response to the interpersonal relationships in the family.

I would be remiss, however, if I did not emphatically state that one's interpersonal relationships do affect one's biology. These relationships can impact an individual who is ill in both negative and positive ways. Relationships have been proven to be a hindrance to healing or treatment, as well as a tremendous healing resource for a sick family member. As a relationship therapist, I have known this for decades. Many therapists and others have intuited and observed this to be true. Now we have "scientific" proof.

I have long appreciated and been fascinated with the work of psychiatrist Daniel Siegel. His research validates the importance that the quality of significant relationships have on one's health and well-being.[2]

In the past several decades, information from the field of neuroscience has helped us to understand the connection between mind, body, and relationships. This important research has created more and more treatment options, which are being explored in all aspects of treating an individual's biological/chemical, mental, and emotional well-being.

Triangles with Extended Family

When working with couples, it is common to discover that a source of tension is quite often triangulation with extended family. The In-Law Triangle is probably the most predominate of these. It is a favorite theme often portrayed in movies and written about in books. I write more about the In-Law Triangle in chapter 6, which discusses the issue of loyalty and legacy. The primary goal when working with a couple dealing with in-law issues is to help the couple create a safe and trusting bond with each other, so that it is safe for each of them to make the other, and not their parents, the primary bond. The individuals in the couple can hopefully do this in a way that does not harm the relationship each has with his/her parents.

Interlocking Triangles

In a family system, there are many combinations of triangles operating at the same time. Many of these triangles are interlocking; that is, one or more of the persons in one triangle may be simultaneously in other triangles. Here is an example of interlocking triangles:

Mary is a forty-year-old nun, and is devoted to her Catholic faith. She is a loving daughter to her widowed mother. She is very close to her younger sister, Sarah, and an adoring aunt to Sarah's daughter, Holly, age fifteen.

Sarah and her mother, Holly's grandmother, are in constant arguments about everything, particularly about how Sarah parents Holly. They each try to enlist Mary to be on their side.

Holly, Mary's niece, is often at odds with her mother and grandmother and often goes to her Aunt Mary for help in dealing with the other two. Holly often wants Mary to intervene. Even though Mary is a nun, Holly experiences Mary as much more open-minded than her mother or grandmother.

Let's take a look at the triangles.

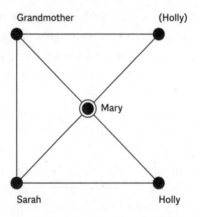

5.2. Intergenerational and interlocking triangles

Mary may enjoy being in these family triangles. She may experience feeling important and connected. She may value the impact that she has on her other family members, which gives her a sense of belonging as well as power. If this is the case, then her being triangulated is not likely doing any harm to her. However, if Mary or any of the other family members experience the triangle alliances as negative rather than positive, then there would be a problem.

Every family has sets of interlocking triangles. These may change form over time, or they may stay rigidly in place. But, as with all triangles, they exist as a means to stabilize the system in some way.

Triangulation Beyond Family Members

Thus far, I have focused on triangulation in which a dyad chooses a person to be in the triangle. This is done to ease the anxiety of at least one of the members of the dyad. The person or persons are generally not consciously aware that they are attempting to reduce their anxiety by triangulating the third person. Often the person being triangulated by one or both individuals in a dyad is a child. The triangulated person can also be a parent, a sibling, a friend, or a lover.

Two people may choose to ease the anxiety experienced by each or both by triangulating a job, a hobby, religion, or a pet. In this day and age, individuals use their computers and especially their cell phones.

One of the most common complaints I hear from couples is that their partner is not available. I always hear this as both physical and *emotional* unavailability. They are usually referring to the fact that the *other person* works too much, plays too much golf, spends all their time helping friends, taking care of the kids, working in the yard, or on their cell phones. I hear this as an individual's attempt to avoid conflict or intimacy or BOTH (I believe that we cannot have true intimacy without conflict). Triangulating something or someone beyond the immediate or extended family is, again, the individual's attempt to reduce their anxiety.

Triangulation occurs repeatedly and extensively throughout the life cycle of the family and across the generations. The experience of triangulating a third person or thing may be a brief solution, or a constant. It may have a minor effect on the family members or a devastating effect on one or more of the members.

Devastation occurs when the triangle becomes rigid, and the individuals are "locked" into this triad experience for years or decades. Birth order, sibling position, and gender often dictate which child (or children) may be chosen to be triangulated into the spousal subsystem.

Birth Order

While studying Adlerian psychology in graduate school, I found Alfred Adler's Birth Order Theory interesting. However, I have found that there are ALWAYS exceptions to these birth-order attributes. I have encountered the "exceptions" more often than not. That being stated, I have decided to include them because there is almost always a grain of truth in these ideas, and because birth order and sibling position are often an important frame of reference when examining a family system.

Long before the development of Family Systems Theory, Alfred Adler, who was a contemporary of Sigmund Freud, developed theories of personality that focused on understanding an individual within the context of his birth order in his family.

Heinz Ansbacher, a German-American psychologist, and his wife, Rowena Ansbacher, wrote the following about birth order as was asserted in Adlerian psychology:

> Adler postulated that the oldest child is often prone to the
> need for affirmation and approval. Adler attributes this
> to the child losing the parents' undivided attention once
> another child is born and compensates throughout life by
> working to get it back. First-born children are often good

at relating to adults and tend to be productive through-out their lives. They may be expected to set an example and be given responsibility for younger siblings.

Adler describes the second-born child as being more competitive, and rebellious. Middle children sometimes struggle with figuring out their place in the family. They are eager for parental praise and may excel in music or sports, to accomplish this goal. They may more easily adapt to change and be more diplomatic than the oldest or youngest child.

In Adler's theory, the youngest child may be selfish and dependent. The youngest child may be free to have fun and often enjoys being the center of attention while enjoying entertaining others. Youngest children often express confidence and ease in relating to others and are often successful because of their relationship skills.

Adler described only children as tending to take on the traits of the oldest or youngest child. Since only children do not have to share their parents' attention, they may have a difficult time sharing with others or being told no.

Adler, when comparing only children to others their age, observed that only children are often more mature and feel more comfortable around adults and tend to do better in intellectual and creative endeavors.[3]

It is important to remember that gender, class, age difference, and temperament are a few of the variables that influence the impact of birth order on an individual's experience in the family.

All the birth order positions have plusses and minuses. Knowing what these are and activating one's choice potentially allows for transcending any limitations that may be inherent in the sibling position. The more individuals can think and feel their own thoughts and feelings separate from those of their families, the more available the choice potential.

Triangulation often occurs when a child is in the same sibling position as was the parent of the same sex. A parent may over-identify with this child. A mother who was the youngest child and felt vulnerable by virtue of being such may find herself always sticking up for her youngest daughter when she thinks another one of the other children are picking on her. This mother may attempt to rescue her youngest daughter when she thinks her husband is being too critical or punishing. She may overly bond with this child, often using this child to maintain distance from her spouse.

George and Sue came in with their youngest daughter, Beth. Beth had been caught smoking in the girl's restroom at school and had been suspended. George began explaining that he had been upset with Beth for several months because she was not following the rules. He said he was upset with Sue not only because she refused to back him up but because she fought with him about how to handle Beth's "bad" behavior. I observed Beth and Sue engaged in eye-rolling behavior as George, heatedly, shared *the problem.*

I learned that Sue was the youngest daughter of a raging alcoholic father. I also learned that George's and Sue's second child, and only son, had left for college three months earlier. George said he misses his son, and that he found it frustrating to be the only male in the house. It soon became clear that George and Sue had used the children to fill the void their distancing from each other had created. They each seemed equally fearful of intimacy. Sue got her intimacy needs met in her overly close relationship with Beth. Sue found George's attempts to get closer to her, since the departure of their son, threatening. Sue's attempt to pull Beth in closer met with rebellion from Beth. Beth's acting-out behavior was an attempt to establish her growing up and separating from her family. Sue sided with her daughter as an attempt to stay close to Beth, thus avoiding intimacy with George.

Once again, couple therapy was recommended. As is often the case, children "bring" their parents for therapy!

As has been stated previously, the more rigid the triangles, the more devastating they are to the individual(s). Rigid triangles usually are ones that remain constant over many years. They are sometimes referred to as the "central" or "dominant" family triangle. This dominant triangle usually takes precedence over all other triangles in the family system. It most often includes persons from different generations. It may, and usually does, repeat over the generations.

It is not unusual for the dominant familial triangle to contain a parentified child or a troubled or scapegoated child. These roles can be passed from one child to another.

I remember how astounded I was when I first realized this phenomenon in my practice. One family comes to mind; I will call them the Taylor family. Mr. and Mrs. Taylor came in reluctantly with their children: Kevin (17), Tim (14), and Billy (9). I say reluctantly because they wanted me to meet only with Kevin. After all, they explained, Kevin was "the problem." Kevin had been skipping school with a group of friends and they had found some pot in his book bag.

They wanted me to "fix" Kevin. After giving the parents only a few minutes to trash Kevin, I asked my typical question to ALL the family members (I required all to be present at the first session). The question was, "If you could change your family in some way to be more how you would like it, what would that be?"

I decided to start with Billy, the youngest.

Billy: "I would like to have a dog. . . . (elaborates). And I would like for Dad to be home more so that we could play ball."

Tim: "I would like to not have to come here. (laughter) I would like to go to the mall with my friends. (pause) I would like for Mom and Dad to stop fighting."

(Complete silence)

Kevin: (emerging from a slump and pulling the baseball cap away from covering his eyes) "I want more freedom. I want Mom to stop nagging me and Dad to get off my case. School is boring. Everyone smokes pot. I don't know what the big deal is. Besides, Dad, what right do you have to talk? You are out late every night drinking with your buddies."

It is obvious at this point that the "problem" is not only Kevin's behavior. There is also a marital problem and a substance abuse problem with one or more of the family members.

I scheduled a session to meet with the parents without the children. I suggested they do some couple therapy. Neither one was open to the idea of couple therapy. They were adamant that they were only coming in to therapy because of their son, Kevin. So I did some family therapy and worked with them around parenting Kevin: limit-setting and defining and enforcing consequences, etc. The situation improved, and they disappeared from therapy.

One year later the Taylor family returned. They reported that Kevin graduated "by the skin of his teeth." He was attending a nearby junior college and had moved into an apartment with a friend. He was working part-time.

Now, Tim was "the problem." Tim had been caught defacing public property and he was put on probation. What brought them in, however, was the fact that Tim had become physically violent at home. He was throwing things and had recently put his fist through the kitchen wall.

I asked him to describe this incident to me in detail. I noticed Tim seemed extremely despondent.

> **Tim began:** "We had just finished dinner. Mom was upset because, once again, Dad didn't make it home for dinner. I made a comment about how he loved his booze more than us. She got mad and said that he might want to be home more if it weren't for me, that I was such a disappointment to him. That my being on probation was the worst thing that had ever happened to him. I lost it! I started yelling at her. Just then Dad walked in the door. He started yelling at me. I wanted to punch HIM. But I hit the wall instead and walked out."

I observed Billy's tears as Tim was telling his story. This time I was not willing to NOT confront the parents. They were unwittingly setting up their sons, one by one, to act out and take the rap for their marital problems and Dad's alcohol problem.

In classic family therapy, we would call this a *reframe*, a therapeutic intervention that challenges a family's perception by calling the symptom or behavior something different and altering the context in which it is perceived by the family. The family presents a problem to the therapist. For example, Kevin has or is THE PROBLEM. The family therapist reframes the problem from "Kevin has/is the problem" to "the family system is dealing with some tension and stress, and Kevin is the person in the family who is expressing this stress and tension by being the 'symptom bearer.'"

Kevin's parents did not accept this reframe when they came in the first time with Kevin as "the problem." However, when they came in with their second son, Tim, they were more amenable to considering that the problem was not only with Tim (previously Kevin) but also in the marital relationship.

I agreed to work with the family, but insisted the couple get into marriage therapy with one of my colleagues. They complied.

I was convinced that Billy was the next to be scapegoated if the parents did not do their therapy work. The family worked diligently in therapy. Billy did not get triangulated as the next scapegoat.

They stopped family therapy after ten months. Hopefully, the parents were successful in doing their work in couple therapy, and the father dealt with his alcohol abuse. If not, Billy may have become triangulated as a parentified child (aligning with his mother and becoming her confidant). Families don't usually see this as a problem and therefore do not seek therapy.

In summary, triangles are inevitable. They may be brief and functional, causing no harm, or they may be rigid and long-term, causing harm to one or more of the individuals in the system.

Recognizing the triangles and observing their functions gives us the power to stay engaged or to disengage. If you are a parent and are triangulating a child, I urge you to explore different ways of dealing with the stress or pain you are attempting to alleviate.

Family Triangles

1. Can you identify any triangles in your family? If so, draw them. Were/are you in the triangle? During what part of your life? How did/do you feel about being triangulated?

2. If this was in the past, how did you get out? If in the present, do you want out? If the answer is yes, how can you imagine doing so?

3. If you were not triangulated, but observed others being in a triangle, how did that make you feel?

4. If you are a parent, identify a time you or your partner drew a child into a triangle with each other. (Every parent does so at some point in time.) Do you know what purpose that served for you or your partner? Have you or your partner "released" the child (children) from this triangle?

5. What triangles can you identify in your mother's and father's families?

6. Do you recognize any triangles repeating over the generations?

Triangulation Beyond Family Members

1. Can you identify any triangles in your family of origin or your current family that involve something or someone, not a family member? If so, how did/ does this triangle attempt to address the anxiety experienced by one or more of the family members?

(Note: If someone in the family is a philanderer, the reasons for this person's behavior may go way beyond the normal desire to mitigate anxiety. This is not a subject addressed in this book. I suggest readings by Frank Pittman.)

Chapter Six

Who Owes What to Whom?

Family Loyalty, Legacy, and Ledger

All I am or hope to be I owe to my mother.
ABRAHAM LINCOLN

One of the early family systems theorists, Ivan Boszormenyi-Nagy, postulated that families create obligations, expectations, debts, entitlements, and responsibilities among their members.

He asserted that every family maintains a family ledger, *an interpersonal/relational account book* of who owes what to whom, and that this ledger spans across the generations. This family ledger is composed of demanded and perceived loyalties as well as conscious and unconscious debts owed (which may or may not be related to monetary issues), but also includes what the individuals believe they are due and what they are required to give relationally.

An important component of the family ledger is the concept of *legacy, that which children acquire by being born into their families of origin*. Legacy often implies "destiny," a predetermined way to "be" in the world.

Another important concept in the family ledger is that of loyalty. Individuals are tied to their families by powerful and enduring emotional, physical, and social attachments. One's loyalty to one's family is governed not only by what is known but also by what is unknown to the individual.[1]

Loyalty

Loyalties may fluctuate, but they do persist, often outside an individual's awareness. Loyalty among family members is impacted by the culture in which the family is embedded. Cultural and religious doctrines influence what a family demands of its members in terms of loyalty regarding each member's thoughts and behavior.

Issues of loyalty and legacy are intergenerational ones. That is, they are passed down from one generation to the next . . . and the next. One of the functions of family rules is to prescribe how its members are to be loyal. These overt rules for loyalty can sometimes become problematic for individuals in the family.

A good example of an overt family rule that may become problematic is that of a male who is born into an Italian American mafia family and who wants to escape from the rules and expectations placed on him even before his birth. Stories of the Italian American mafia are some of the more popular examples involving family loyalty and legacy. Most of us have encountered this idea in great detail in movies or books.

The Italian American mafia is portrayed as demanding absolute loyalty from its members. Even though the mafia is called a "family," it is not made up of only biologically related individuals. However, as we have seen portrayed in such films as *The Godfather*, fathers and sons, nephews and uncles can indeed be a part of this organization. The individual male who is expected to follow in the legacy and to be loyal to the "family business" but decides to follow another path may be highly criticized, judged, or expelled by his family, even murdered.

Although extreme, these portrayals are good examples of the depth of the issues that may arise out of the power of loyalty and legacy expectations in a family. We all struggle with the issue of what our family expects from us and our need for individuality.

I have seen the issue of loyalty and legacy show up in therapy when an individual desires to break from "tradition." An example is the Catholic or Jewish person who wants to marry out of his or her faith when the family rule is that one ONLY marries a person who shares the same tradition and religion as one's family.

In the past decade, more and more of my clients have presented with the relational difficulties that arise out of the social and political issues currently at large in the country and the world. Most of the relational struggles are with family members who hold different points of view. For many families, these struggles are an attack on the concept of loyalty and legacy that have been in operation for generations in their families.

Legacy

We are each born into a family that has its own set of rules, values, and beliefs. We are all impacted by these rules, values, and beliefs. Children who are raised in families that put a high value on independence and autonomy are generally more able to decide which of their family rules, values, and beliefs they want to hold onto and which ones they choose to no longer accept and abide. If the family promotes the concept of "free to disagree," then relational ruptures are less likely to occur in the family system.

In families that demand that all their members hold the same rules, values, and beliefs, cutoffs may occur when a family member chooses to follow a different path in beliefs and actions. The examples I experience most often around this have to do with religion, politics, and prejudice around race, sexual orientation, and gender identity issues. It always hurts my heart when I hear of someone being disowned by their family because of what this individual believes and who they are.

It has not been uncommon for familial legacies to relate to gender. Females are to be teachers or nurses. Male children are to be engineers. Males are to be strong and not express emotion. Females are not to be athletic. This list could go on and on. Some of this may sound much more ridiculous now than it did in the middle of the last century. However, gender legacies still exist.

Just recently I was working with a thirty-five-year-old single white female. The familial legacy in her family was that females were to marry and have children. Male children, however, need not marry and produce offspring. The male children were expected to become very successful financially. Her family considered my client a disappointment and a "failure." Though she was a CEO of a major corporation, her family did not accept her as successful because she was not married with children.

The Devastating Legacy of Suicide

Perhaps the saddest of legacies is that of the legacy of suicide. In one of the numerous studies that took place in the 1990s regarding the repetition of suicide among family members, Kendler et al. revealed that a family who has experienced a completed suicide significantly increases the risks of suicide attempts by other family members.[2]

There are numerous hypotheses about why the risk of suicide is greater in a family that has had a suicide. Suicidal tendencies are not hereditary; however, mental illness is. If a suicide in a family is related to clinical depression, then other family members might have the genetic disposition to be depressed. It would be important for the individual suffering with depression to seek help. Medication would likely be recommended, along with talk therapy.

Another hypothesis is that once a family member completes suicide, then suicide becomes an "option" for others if one is unhappy or struggling in some way. There have also been instances when a family member decides to commit suicide to attempt to reconcile confusion or diminish the pain of missing the deceased family member. Survivor guilt is not uncommon. An individual may decide to attempt suicide because that person believes that he should have been the one to die. It is not only despair and hopelessness that lead to acts of suicide but also the desire to relieve some feelings of guilt or shame.

It is important for families who have experienced a death by suicide to be emotionally available to one another and to seek help and support.

Legacy of Grieving

Most families have rules about how their members are to grieve, particularly around the death of one of their members. For some families, the process of grieving is well-rooted in their religious traditions. In Jewish families, there is the custom of sitting shiva. This is a time when the bereaved family formally mourns their loved one for a period of seven days, typically sitting close to the floor as a symbol of being "brought low" by their sorrow. During this time, friends often visit the family to offer their condolences, typically bringing food for the mourners. In many Irish Catholic families, there may be a wake. A wake is attended by family and friends and is often in the home of the deceased. This is a time when they eat food and drink and share memories of the deceased. Unlike for a traditional funeral service, a religious leader may or may not be present. The term *wake* comes from the old custom of family and friends staying up with the body all night. Historically, the wake occurs before the formal funeral service. In more recent times, the wake may occur after the funeral and/or function more like a memorial service for the deceased.

These traditions prescribe a grieving process that is shared by family and community. There are families, however, where grieving the passing of one of their members is not a shared experience, even among the family members themselves.

To my dismay, my family is one of the latter ones. I learned very early that it was not okay to express deep sorrow when a loved one passes from this earth. I was seven when I first encountered the death of a family member: my grandfather died. I remember being with my parents, aunt and uncle, my brother, my sister, and cousins. My grandmother, Bobba, was in the next room. When we children were told of our grandfather's death, I began sobbing. The tears were streaming down my face, and I was making wailing sounds. My cousin, four years my senior, said to me in a very demanding voice, "Stop crying. You will upset Bobba." Just then, Bobba entered the room. I immediately swallowed my tears and stifled my sobbing sounds. Within minutes my nose started to bleed. My nose bled for three days. I was unable to attend the funeral.

I got the message loud and clear: keep your mourning private. (This experience was my first lesson that emphasized the powerful connection between emotions and physical health.)

Bobba was in her mid-nineties when she died. We had a small funeral.

For many individuals, the gathering with others in remembrance and saying goodbye is important. Death is a rite of passage. For most humans, finding a way to honor this passage with others provides support and closure. Of course, grieving the loss of a loved one does not stop once the shared experience has come to an end. Depending on the relationship one has with the deceased, the grief process will continue.

Grief as a Process

I have always shared with my clients that grieving is a *process*. In her book *On Death and Dying*, Elizabeth Kübler-Ross shared with the world what she identified as five stages of grief. Her observations were focused on people who were in the process of dying. She observed the five stages of grief as being those of denial, bargaining, anger, depression, and acceptance. These stages were common experiences shared by persons who were dying and those close to them. She did not see these stages as a linear process; they did not follow in order, and individuals seemed to move back and forth between the stages.[3]

It is unfortunate that these five stages of grief came to be a model that many people thought was the "right way" to experience the grieving process.

No! No! No! Grieving is a unique process. Every individual experiences it differently.

Except in cases of sudden and devastating loss, we humans can often suffer loss and go along with our lives without much looking different to others on the outside. We can follow through with those tasks we want to do and those that are necessary, like functioning well at our jobs or feeding our children. Since the beginning of time, humans have experienced loss. I think we are inherently programmed to be resilient in the face of loss, even devastating loss.

While this is true, I am always amazed by what a strange creature grief is. I know for me, I can go along functioning normally, not thinking about my loss and allowing myself to be fully present for others. And then a moment arrives, seemingly out of nowhere. It may be in a week, a month, a year, or a decade since the loss occurred. But something happens that triggers my grief, and GRIEF swallows me whole for seconds or minutes.

This kind of sadness is the one experience that seems always to be present when one is grieving. However, the ways in which individuals express their sadness vary immensely. Sadness is normal. I often think of depression as "stuck sadness." In fact, when clients come in for therapy and tell me that they are depressed, my first thought is, "What is the sadness they are not allowing themselves to experience?"

It is normal for the intensity of this sadness to lessen over time. However, it may never entirely go away. Again, for most of us, after the initial experience of loss, we go in and out of grief. We continue with our normal life activities. We might be having a pretty typical day, and then all of a sudden, grief washes over us. Here's how I describe it to my clients: "It could be ten years after the loss of a loved one. You are going along in your normal life, and then suddenly, out of nowhere, a wave of grief comes along like a tsunami and pulls you into an intense moment of experiencing deep loss."

For instance, my beloved grandmother, Bobba, always made homemade hot cross buns on Good Friday. I couldn't wait to walk into her home and smell them cooking. Once they came out of the oven, she would let me put on the icing, in the shape of a cross, on top of the buns. This is a sweet memory for me. Once I left for college, however, I never again was there to smell and eat her homemade hot cross buns.

About eight years after her death, I was driving past a bakery near my office that advertised hot cross buns on Good Friday. I decided to pick some up and take them home so that my sons could experience freshly made hot cross buns. Mind you, I was in my early forties at this time. I walked into the crowded bakery, and immediately upon smelling the baking hot cross buns, I unexpectedly, began sobbing uncontrollably. I was stunned; I had to leave and go sit in my car. At that moment, the tsunami of grief got me. I missed my grandmother so much. After about ten minutes, the intensity of my grief subsided. As embarrassed as I was, I pulled myself together and went back into the bakery to buy the buns.

I often share this tsunami of grief story with my clients, both to clarify that it is important to go on with your life once you've had a great loss, and that grief can be triggered unexpectedly—and that it is okay to let yourself experience the fullness of your sadness, even years after the loss occurred.

What's Money Got to Do With It?

The word *legacy* often conjures up the notion of something being passed from generation to generation, often having to do with social status and money. Oh, what a hornet's nest this issue can be among family members. When it comes to who gets what in terms of the inheritance of money and property, the subject of entitlement and indebtedness can create disagreement, distress, and can endanger the quality of relationships. How inheritance is handled in a family can determine if the family members will stay connected or become so distanced that they never reestablish connection.

Money issues in the extended family go beyond inheritance. Who helps whom when financial difficulties are present? How are the relationships impacted? If a parent needs physical and/or financial assistance, who takes that on, and how is it related to the idea of indebtedness or individual role? Again, loyalty and legacy come into play here.

Money is often used to manipulate and control, reward, and punish. An adult child may feel entitled to or perhaps grateful for a parent's financial assistance or gifts. The adult child may also feel trapped and burdened in relating to a parent in a way that is not in alignment with that individual's true self. The adult child may feel embarrassed or ashamed that the parent is helping financially. A parent, grandparent, sibling, or other relative may feel resentful that an adult child is needy financially.

How couples and families deal with the issue of money can be complicated. When I first started in the field of family therapy, I heard something that has always stayed with me and has rung true. The Big Five issues that couples present in therapy are around sex, chores, together-time, in-laws and MONEY!

As I have stated previously, in dealing with any of these couple issues or other family issues, it is important to *listen, really listen* to one another, attempt to *understand* what the other(s) is/are thinking and feeling, and be willing to *cooperate* when negotiating.

What's in a Name?

Years ago, I heard a Native American describe how his ancestors made introductions to strangers. They introduced themselves by saying, "My maternal grandmother (or grandfather) is _____. My paternal grandmother (or grandfather) is _____." This fascinated me. To identify themselves, they needed to name and acknowledge their ancestors.

Many of us have ancestors who immigrated to the United States, and in so doing were either given or selected a different surname than the one they had in the "old" country. I am always interested in the stories around this occurrence. If I am working with a client, I want them to think about what this means to them. Do they have any feelings about this changing of the family name?

On a related topic, the women's movement gave my generation permission for women to retain their "maiden" name rather than adopt their husband's surname at the time of their marriage. If I am seeing a couple and the wife wants to use her family name instead of her husband's name, I want to understand each of their thoughts and feelings surrounding that decision, to help them resolve any feelings that may inhibit them from forming a secure attachment. Same-sex couples who marry may struggle with this issue as well. Many couples prefer hyphenating their families' names, thus creating new surnames for each of them.

Learning why an individual in a family is given a particular name is often very telling when exploring the issue of legacy. Some children are given names by their parents simply because the parents like the particular name and the name, in and of itself, has no "strings attached." Some children are given names out of a family "tradition"—for example, that all firstborn sons are named after the father. This tradition may carry expectations for the child, or it may not.

There are individuals whose given names carry heavy meanings, expectations, and obligations. An example is a family who came to therapy consisting of a father, a mother, a girl (age six) and a boy (age three). The presenting problem was that the daughter, Diana, was exhibiting self-harming behaviors. She was biting herself on her arm. She would periodically pull out her hair. Her pediatrician had recommended family therapy.

I met with the whole family for the first session. Because of the children's ages, I decided to meet with only the parents to obtain an extensive family history. In doing so, I learned that the parents had married when they were each eighteen and were married for fifteen years before having Diana. I asked why they waited fifteen years to start a family. The mother responded by looking down and avoiding eye contact. The father shared with me that they had had a little girl soon after they were married, who died in a car accident while riding with a neighbor when she was six. Her name was Diana.

The Diana sitting in my office was a "replacement" child.

I hypothesized that there were at least two primary reasons for this little girl to be engaging in self-harm behavior. The first hypothesis was that the "new" Diana unconsciously questioned if she was worthy to be alive. Somewhere deep inside her, outside of conscious awareness, she wondered if her parents wished that the first Diana was alive instead of her.

The second hypothesis was that her mother was becoming increasingly anxious out of fear that her little girl, who was now the same age as the first Diana, might be taken from her. It is my firm belief, born out of my experience, that children often exhibit anxiety that is carried by a parent (Yes, children intuit these things!).

So, our work was twofold. I decided to see the mother both individually and some with her husband. I worked with the mother on dealing with her anxiety by supporting her in processing her grief and healing from the trauma of losing her first child. I worked with the couple to heal the residual relational wound that is experienced by couples when they lose a child (although this couple was in a much better place than most). I helped the parents become aware of why and how they needed to reassure and promote positive self-worth in their living daughter. The daughter's symptoms disappeared fairly quickly once I began working with the mother and the couple.

I am always amazed at how often children unconsciously develop symptoms in order to get their parents into therapy!

A name may carry a blessing or a curse. It may provide a sense of belonging and pride. It may provide a connection and even levity. My name is Elaine. My father's only sibling was a younger sister named Helen. Aunt Helen wanted my mother and father to name me after her. My father was not taken with the idea. My mother wanted to be loyal to my father and honor his wishes, but she also wanted to please my aunt, the only "sister" she'd ever had. My mother and my aunt compromised by using the French form of Helen—Elaine.

I was very fond of my aunt, who was a big part of my life. I have always liked my name. In the small town in which I grew up, I was the only Elaine. (Also, Elaine is the name of the lover of Lancelot. She was the mother of Galahad. As a teenager, I became fascinated with the Arthurian legend. So, I loved my name even more.)

I was, however, the only girl in my school that did not have a middle name. I was jealous that the other girls got to have both a first and middle name. When I asked my mother why I did not get to have a middle name, she explained that she hated her first and middle names. She hated her name so much that she did not give my sister or me middle names. What we were told was that if we did not like our given names, we could choose a name that we liked, and that name would become our legal middle name and the name we could be called if we preferred it to our given name. My sister, Christine, and I both like our given names; neither of us wanted to be called by another name.

Knowing how individuals got their names can be illuminating as to how they are connected to their families and how they think about who they are in the world.

Invisible Loyalties

As problematic as overt family rules demanding loyalty can be, it is the *invisible loyalties*, Boszormenyi-Nagy claimed, that often wreak the most havoc within a family. Individuals may be harmed by loyalty expectations that have been assigned to them in a process that is usually unconscious. Thus, the demand for loyalty is occurring out of one's awareness and is often destructive to the individual's health and well-being. These invisible, unconscious loyalties stretch across generations and influence present behavior.

A mother brought her fifteen-year-old son, Ben, to therapy because she was deeply concerned that he had started drinking alcohol. She called to schedule a session for him after finding him throwing up one night when he had returned home from going out with friends. He told her he usually just drank "a little bit," but that that night he just couldn't stop.

As usual, when she called to schedule the first appointment, I told her that I wanted her to come in with him. No other persons were living in the home, or I would have invited them in, as well.

Ben shared that he was concerned about his drinking. He said that his mother had been upset when she first found out he was drinking. He, however, had not been concerned until the night when he got drunk and became sick.

Ben told me that his father and mother had gotten divorced when he was seven. As is my practice, I asked him why he believed his parents got divorced. He stated that he believed his parents divorced because his father was a "raging" alcoholic. He said that he no longer had contact with his father. After the divorce, his father periodically visited him, but he had not heard from his father during the past three years. He occasionally got news of his father from his aunt, his father's sister, who lived in another state. In the last phone conversation with his aunt, he had learned that his grandfather, his father's father, had died. His aunt told Ben about the grandfather's alcoholism. Ben was aware that his father and grandfather had been estranged, but he was not aware of his grandfather's alcoholism. Ben had only met the grandfather once and did not remember him.

As I engaged in taking a family history, I asked Ben what he remembered about living with his father. He began sharing memories of his father's drinking and his parents' fighting.

I asked him if he had any "good" memories. He began sharing memories of when he was four and five. He had some "good" memories, which he seemed pleased to recall and share with me. He then said something that I realized was key to resolving the "presenting problem"—Ben's alcohol abuse.

As he was sharing fond memories of his father and a time when he felt happy in his family of three, he said: "Everyone used to tell me that I was just like my father. My father was outgoing and funny. The life of the party."

We all sat in silence for a minute. I then asked, "Ben, I am wondering if there is another way for you to connect with and honor the father you carry inside of you, other than abusing alcohol?" He got it!

As we continued working together (and I did see him for a few individual sessions), he was able to detach from the legacy of being "just like" his father. He was able to honor those attributes he liked about his father and himself. He was able to grieve the loss of having a loving, supportive, fun-loving father—something he had never done out of fear that if he grieved losing his father, he would be betraying his mother! His mother was able to reassure him that this was not the case, thus giving him the permission he needed to openly grieve.

We also explored the intergenerational patterns of legacy regarding alcohol abuse and estrangements. I helped him to understand that alcoholism tends to be a generational problem. In his case, both his father and his father's father abused alcohol, thus indicating that he could have a predisposition for abusing alcohol. Ben's father was estranged from his father, as Ben and his father are currently estranged, or cut off from having an ongoing relationship.

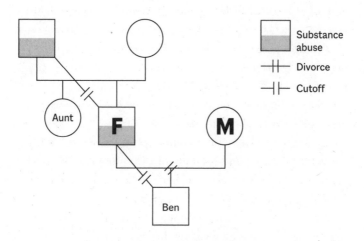

6.1. Genogram depicting intergenerational substance abuse and patterns of cutoffs

Recognizing intergenerational patterns can help individuals understand more about why they are who they are and do what they do. I do not doubt that as a child living with both parents during the ending of their marriage and ultimate divorce, Ben experienced what Nagy refers to as *split filial loyalty*. Nagy believed this to be one of the most problematic forms of loyalty issues. The child is pulled by one or both parents to side with one parent over the other. This dynamic almost always causes the child intrapsychic distress.

I have often witnessed children who react to being in the devastating position of split filial loyalty by suffering from severe emotional and psychological distress. The psychological distress may show up as low self-esteem, becoming withdrawn and depressed, exhibiting "bad" behavior, and even suicidal ideation. Parents, please refrain from putting your children in this position! Children will often put themselves in this position; they don't need a parent to intensify what they are already doing to themselves.

Unfortunately, parents are not the only culprits who may demand split filial loyalty. Grandparents may enlist a child to join with them against a parent or another grandparent. In each of these above scenarios, a child has been triangulated by an adult family member.

Family loyalty and legacy often weigh heavily on an individual, demanding they think and behave as the family dictates. It takes courage for an individual to claim their own thoughts and beliefs if those differ from what their family thinks and believes. It takes courage and determination to act on those differences.

The Family Ledger

As I have stated previously, in addition to family legacy and loyalty, each member of a family has a ledger of entitlements and indebtedness. Nagy describes the imbalance of the ledger early in a child's life, stating that the young child is entitled to be taken care of by his/her parents. Normally, the parents do not expect the child to be indebted to them for this. However, as the child grows into adulthood, more responsibilities and indebtedness develop. If a child is expected to take on more responsibility than she is developmentally prepared to do, then this child will likely experience emotional and psychological distress.

The number of individuals I have seen in my practice who deal with issues of "balancing" the ledger is high. It shows up in adult clients as "wanting what they deserve." Or, on the flip side, feeling the need to take care of a parent or grandparent. This is not necessarily destructive. It is indeed a way of balancing the ledger. It may become destructive if the individual becomes sacrificial to the point of self-destruction, or if a parent is demanding to be repaid without any regard to the impact on the adult child. The phrase, "I took care of you, now it is your turn to take care of me" can be an attempt by a parent of robbing their adult child from living her own life. I have seen so many individuals put their lives "on hold" while being caretakers for other family members.

Taking care of family members is often necessary. Making sacrifices is an essential part of being in relationships. However, choosing to make sacrifices is not the same as choosing to be "sacrificial." Choosing to be "sacrificial" (i.e., denying one's own wants and needs) is destructive to one's self and the relationship. Being a martyr is rarely beneficial. And yet, some individuals seem to be drawn to martyr themselves.

Parents often project onto a child a debt that they believed is owed them from their family of origin or their spouse. A single mother whose father left her as a young child may project onto her son the debt of her father for abandoning her. She may not want this child to leave home. If he does, she may follow him from place to place.

A father who had to take care of his younger sister when he was a young boy may project onto his daughter the debt of his sister and his mother for needing him to take care of the sister; thus expecting the daughter to take care of him.

Issues of ledger and squabbling over who owes what to whom can also occur between siblings, as well as between spouses and couples in a committed relationship. It is not uncommon for individuals in a marriage to attempt to collect debts from their spouses which were owed to them from their families of origin. This sets forth unrealistic expectations and creates resentment, which can rupture the intimate bond.

I have sat with many couples in therapy when one will go on and on about what they have given or not received from the other. It is obvious that the individual is keeping a ledger. Individuals in a couple often keep a ledger recording the "deeds of wrongdoing" of the other. They then like to whip out this document, literally or metaphorically, each time they get into a fight with their partners. We therapists often refer to this as *brown-bagging*.

Loyalty, legacy, and ledger issues are frequently the basis for problems in a marriage. Developmental transitions require individuals to become aware and to deal with the issues of loyalty to their family of origin. Marriage is the most demanding of these transitions.

Individuals carry an often-undefined loyalty to their parents and ancestors. It certainly is not uncommon for individuals to choose a marriage partner because of the family from which this person comes. Whether in the movies or real life, we have all heard such phrases as:

"She is marrying into a good family."

"He is marrying above his station."

In a slightly different vein, I have had clients who are more attached (and therefore more loyal) to their spouse's family than to the spouse. This often becomes most apparent when the couple is getting a divorce. I have witnessed clients crying at the thought of losing their partner's family but who are content with losing their partner.

In-Law Loyalty Triangles

Because I believe that family triangles involving in-laws are born out of *loyalty* issues as well as intimacy issues, I have included them in this chapter rather than chapter 5, which discussed triangles in the family system in great detail.

The marital bond assumes that spouses will transition their primary attachment from their parent(s) to their spouse. This can be a very difficult shift for some individuals who maintain a deep sense of loyalty to a parent or to their family of origin. If the transition takes place successfully, the relationship with one's parents remains important but is no longer the individual's primary attachment.

In the course of reading a book called *The Evaluation and Treatment of Marital Conflict: A Four-Stage Approach*, I was intrigued with the identifying and naming of three common in-law triangles.[4] I have come to identify the three most prevalent in-law family triangles as the following:

Idealized Father Triangle

We see this when the wife's father gets more loyalty and respect than she gives her husband, and the husband cannot possibly live up to the wife's idealized father. The wife calls on her father for advice and guidance. The wife's father often takes great pleasure in being this important to his daughter and encourages her dependency on him. He may even openly demand this loyalty, withholding love and support if he is not given this loyalty.

This triangle may not only be wife/father and husband but also husband/father and wife. The husband and his father may be "peas in a pod." The husband relies on his father for companionship and support. In this case, the wife is the outsider. In cases where the husband works for the family business, his father may also be his boss, adding another dimension of importance of father over wife.

Mother Is My Best Friend Triangle
The same dynamics of the previous triangle play out between spouses here, except with the mother in the role of the third member of the triangle. This triangle seems to be more prevalent between mothers and daughters than sons and mothers, although I have witnessed both sons and daughters who share much more about their most vulnerable selves with their mothers rather than their partners.

With This Family, I Thee Wed Triangle
In this triangle, the wife may be giving her father to her husband, or her husband to her father. After all, her father always wanted a son, or maybe her husband didn't have a father in the picture, and is longing for a father figure. If the wife's loyalty is to her father and she wants to be close to him, this strategy may backfire, because her father may enjoy being more connected to her husband than to her. Whether she is gifting her father to her husband or her husband to her father, she may also be hoping their connection gives her some breathing room from her father and/or her husband.

The *With This Family, I Thee Wed* triangle also gets played out when the husband gives his mother to his wife. (This seems to occur more frequently than the wife giving her mother to her husband.) The wife/mother-in-law/husband triangle allows the husband to disconnect from his mother and remain loyal to her. It is not unusual when this triangle is in operation to see the wife and mother-in-law spending time together socially, joining together to raise the children and care for other family members, and to both "mother" the husband.

Parents-in-law are not the only in-law triangles. Siblings may also be triangulated in a couple's relationship. I recall the song "Sisters" by Irving Berlin from the movie *White Christmas*. The song is sung by two sisters whose relationship is so close that they warn their prospective suitors to beware that no man should try to come between them. It is true that some sisters and brothers experience the sibling bond as more primary than that of the marital bond. Fortunately, there is another line in the song in which each sister warns the other to avoid coming between themselves and the man with whom they are each interested.

I remind you that the family creates triangles to help mitigate stress and anxiety in one or more of the persons in the family system. Triangles serve a purpose, and are not inherently negative or positive.

In-law triangles focus on the issue of degree of attachment and who has the authority of influence. If either spouse has an overly close relationship with a member of their family of origin, then the other spouse will most likely experience being an outsider. Then if the couple experiences conflict or marital problems, these loyalty bond triangles may make it more difficult for the couple to come back together in their relationship, and can exaggerate a break in the bonding of the couple. As is often the case, once family members become involved in a conflict between spouses, recovery is much more difficult.

Cheryl and David came in for marital therapy. They had been married for ten years and had one child, a seven-year-old daughter. Cheryl called to make the appointment because she and David were fighting all the time since he had lost his job one month earlier. She was angry that he sat on the couch all day instead of looking for another job.

It was immediately obvious to me that David was severely depressed. When David shared his skills and work history, I believed he could easily get employment if he were not so depressed. When I attempted to address David's depression in the second session, Cheryl became agitated. She began saying that his depression was just an excuse, that the problem was that he was just "lazy."

As usual, I asked each of them to share their family histories. Cheryl revealed that she and her mother were very close. She spoke to her mother every day on the phone. Cheryl would share with her mother all the little things David did or did not do that disappointed, hurt, or aggravated her. Cheryl was constantly "making a case" against David, and her mother joined in the chorus of "Ain't he awful."

Until recently when David lost his job, most of the complaints Cheryl shared with her mother were of minor consequence: he forgot to take out the trash; he did not get her flowers for their anniversary; he had to work late and missed a parent/teacher conference. For most of their marriage, she had used her relationship with her mother to voice her grievances against David. So, when this really big crisis of David losing his job emerged, both Cheryl and her mother began hounding him and implying that he was "not good enough." Instead of feeling supported and encouraged by his wife, he felt humiliated and disparaged by both Cheryl and her mother. His response was to withdraw, resulting in his going into a depression that rendered him lethargic and unmotivated to find a job.

Unfortunately, this is not an uncommon scenario. One's loyalty and closeness to one's family of origin can be detrimental to one's relationship with one's partner.

It is also true that an individual's loyalty and legacy to their family can hinder them from fully becoming who they could be.

None of us get past childhood without carrying within us loyalties and legacies inherited from our families. We all have a ledger of entitlements and indebtedness. The more balanced the ledger is with our families, the freer we are to live our lives fully and to engage in intimate relationships with others.

Balancing the ledger may involve forgiving "debts." Not only those "debts" owed to you but those you owe as well. The question to ask is, "What is the cost of forgiving this debt?" If the cost is too great, don't forgive it. Most often, holding onto a debt is greater than the cost of releasing it, particularly if carries emotional energy. It is important to remember that forgiveness is the act of letting go emotionally.

Forgiving does NOT mean forgetting. Forgiveness does not mean letting go of holding yourself or another accountable. The act of forgiving means releasing the emotional energy you have attached to a person or situation. Forgiving is a gift you give yourself.

Identifying the loyalty and legacy issues in one's family of origin can help one to break free from being "bound" to one's family in a way that prohibits psychological freedom and growth. Identifying loyalty and legacy issues can also help promote self-empowerment by encouraging an individual to claim their legacy, rather than being a passive accomplice. For example: A daughter takes over her mother's real estate business because loyalty and legacy demanded her to do so. If the daughter does so from a passive position (i.e., this is what is expected and she does not feel she has a choice), she will likely find herself much less content than if she recognizes that she has a choice to stay or back away. If she chooses to stay rather than "having" to stay, she moves from a place of passive acceptance to one of strength and power.

Claim your choices.
Claim your life.

Who Owes What to Whom?

Family Legacy

1. What was/is your legacy within your family of origin? (example: to be a success, failure, clown, teacher, etc.)

2. Does/did this legacy feel like a blessing or a curse?

3. If you successfully released an unwanted legacy, how did you do so?

4. If you want to release an unwanted legacy, can you imagine what you would need to do?

5. If you are a parent, what legacies are you passing on to your children?

Family Loyalty

1. Can you identify loyalty bonds in your family? Which ones involve you? Do those *loyalty* bonds feel destructive or productive to you?

2. Have you experienced or witnessed examples of *split loyalty*? If so, how has that impacted you?

3. Are there any *invisible loyalties* you can identity? If so, what impact have they had on you?

Family Ledger

1. What is the present status of the *ledger* between you and your parents (be they living or deceased)? What has been given and what is owed?

2. If you are partnered, what is the status of the ledger between the two of you? If this ledger is unbalanced, does this present problems in your relationship? How so?

3. If you have children, think about the ledger that exists between you. Does this seem inhibiting or life-enhancing for you and the child?

Naming

1. Do you know how you got your name? Is it a source of connection or pride? Do you experience your name as a blessing or a curse?

Chapter Seven

Keep or Reveal a Family Secret?

Traversing the Minefield of Family
Secrets—*Dangerous Territory!*

How can we make peace with an internal "demon,"
a parent with whom we have been wounded—
if we don't know the truth?

REBECCA WELLS,
DIVINE SECRETS OF THE YA-YA SISTERHOOD

There is no simple way to deal with this issue. Family members and clinicians struggle with the pros and cons of keeping and revealing secrets.

Secrets kept can cause problems.

Secrets revealed can cause problems.

In this chapter, I explore many different types of secrets that individuals and families hold, and how *shame* is often connected to the carrying of secrets.

The subject of shame is so very important. It will be mentioned in this chapter as it pertains to family secrets. The subject of shame goes way beyond family secrets. However, that is not the focus of this book.

I also distinguish between secrecy and privacy.

Privacy Versus Secrets

Naima Brown-Smith defined a family secret as any information that directly affects or concerns one but is either withheld or differentially shared between or among family members.

According to Brown-Smith, family secrets generally present with these elements:

1. The person or persons holding the secret
2. The person or persons unaware of the secret, but who are impacted by the secret
3. Others who are not directly related to the secret
4. The subject of the secret[1]

One of the reasons dealing with the issue of family secrets is so difficult is because of the often-blurred boundary between one's right to privacy and the impact this private "secret" has on other family members. Both privacy and secrecy conceal information from others. What seems like a "secret" to one individual may not seem so to another.

Individuals and couples certainly have a right to privacy. Without privacy, one may lose some sense of self and well-being. We all have thoughts and feelings that are ours alone and that we do not wish to share.

I remember a friend I had when I was a child. She was the third child in a family of seven children. She shared a room, her clothes, her bath time, and most everything with other members in her family.

One day she asked me if she could share a secret with me. I responded in the affirmative. I followed her into the woods near our homes. We came to a big tree. She stopped and took a spoon out of her pocket. She began digging in the dirt between two large roots of the tree. She then lifted out a small plastic box. In it were hundreds of tiny golden stars; the kind that teachers sometimes would put on our homework when it was worthy. I have never forgotten the look on my friend's face of complete delight and awe: her private secret. I was honored. I continue to be honored with the secrets that my clients and others share with me.

I think of this example as a "benign" secret. In fact, to me, it seems more like she got to have something in her life that was private. She lived in a family where so much had to be shared among the family members that having something she could have privately, separately from the others, was important and healthy.

I encourage you to think about what your family's rules were about honoring a person's privacy and how that influences you in your current relationships.

Both adults and children are entitled to privacy. There has been a lot of concern expressed that in this age of cyberspace technology, it is more and more difficult to have and to maintain privacy. Several years ago, I was visiting a friend. While we were standing in her kitchen, we started talking about her wanting a new refrigerator. She had a new addition in her room that her husband had recently purchased, a virtual assistant technology called Alexa. My friend loved being able to ask Alexa about the weather predictions, and to play certain songs. We neither one realized that Alexa was also listening to our conversations. Later that day, she received lots of emails and pop-up ads on her computer for refrigerators. Yes, indeed, privacy has become more and more difficult in our current age of technology.

Secrets may reside in an individual, a couple, a family household, an extended family, or even a larger contextual system. Family secrets are categorized into *internal family secrets,* in which one or more individuals are keeping a secret from at least one other family member, and *shared family secrets,* in which the family as a whole is keeping the secret from those persons outside the family. We most often see shared family secrets in families where there is substance abuse, physical abuse, and secrets that relate to shame about someone or something that is happening within the family currently or has happened in past generations.

An internal family secret is defined as hidden information that is relevant to those from whom it is being kept. This definition is what separates privacy from secrets. The key word is *relevant*. Some secrets are benign, meaning they do not truly impact another. The secret of my friend who had the buried treasure is an example of a benign secret.

The two most common ways secrets are held in relationships are by lying and by withholding information. When lying, the individual gives false information. When withholding, the individual omits relevant information.

Protecting Self or Protecting Other?

Most of the time an individual holds a secret because that individual believes he has something to lose if certain others knew about the secret, and the individual wants to protect himself. There are also times when the decision to keep a secret has been made because of the desire to "protect" others. Or, we have the situation when one rationalizes that he is keeping a secret to protect others, when it is really only himself he wants to protect.

One of the many services offered by the center where I have practiced therapy for half a century is to counsel individuals who have experienced a loss of a family member by suicide. It is not uncommon for surviving family members to want to keep their loved one's death by suicide a secret—although thankfully, the stigma once associated with suicide has diminished since I first began my practice. I have sat with many clients who have had a family member choose to end their life. The guilt and shame they experience tends to complicate their grieving process. It is out of shame that many do not want others to know the truth about the cause of death of the family member. They often want to protect the memory of the person who has committed suicide, and they want to protect themselves from exposing their shame.

Many parents struggle with whether or not they should share with their children that the deceased family member committed suicide. Again, they may be protecting the memory of the deceased family member. In my experience, these parents also want to protect their children from the emotional impact this information will have on the children. We advocate honesty, though of course, a child's age and developmental stage needs to be considered when choosing what words to use when sharing this information, as well as how much information to share.

I am a strong advocate of an individual's right to privacy. It is my experience that we all carry our own personal secrets. Again, these "secrets" only become problematic when the hidden information is relevant to those from whom it is being kept. A spouse who is currently having a secret affair, for instance, is detrimentally impacting the other spouse and children. This secret is destructive. Destructive secrets eat away at relationship integrity. They are like an undiagnosed cancer. You cannot treat what you do not know is there.

Destructive Secrets

I remember a story a colleague shared many years ago regarding the destructive nature of secrets.

This male colleague had been working with a middle-aged man who presented with severe depression. After working together for several years, the client was much less depressed. For the most part, he was content with his life. They were beginning to discuss termination, even though both the therapist and the client acknowledged that the client still experienced some depression. The client was convinced that this was simply his "lot in life."

Shortly before they were to terminate their work together, the client called in with a severe crisis. He shared that he was having suicidal thoughts and was not sure he wanted to go on living.

As the therapist and client sat together in an emergency session, the client shared that his favorite aunt had just passed away. The client was shocked at the depth of his grief. He and the therapist were even more surprised at the depth of his despair. Something felt "all wrong" to both of them. But what?

Later that week, the client returned at his usual appointment time. His demeanor was completely different. Not only was he not despairing, but his depression had dissipated. The client shared that after the funeral for his beloved aunt, his mother shared with him a family secret.

The secret: the beloved aunt was actually the client's biological mother. The woman who raised him as her son was his mother's older sister. The client shared the details of the secret, and also shared that for the first time in his life, he felt whole. He felt that he finally knew who he was. His mother told him that she and his birth mother, the woman he had thought was his aunt, had planned to tell him when he was 18. But because of other family issues that had occurred at that time, they had decided to wait. His biological mother had then decided that because they had waited so long to tell him, that she wanted to go on keeping the secret from him.

The client expressed his belief that something inside himself "always knew there was something he did not know," and that now "knowing" released him from a deep sadness that he had carried with him throughout his life, which he and his therapist had identified as depression.

In this example, family members had kept a secret to protect another family member. However, that desire to protect became a liability for the individual being protected, an outcome which more often than not is the result of family secrets.

Adults and children (especially children) sense when there is tension or when something does not feel "right." This sensing or knowing creates anxiety in the family members whom the secret impacts but who are consciously unaware of the secret.

It has been my experience that often secrets that are unknown in the conscious mind of the person from whom the secret is being kept are somehow experienced in that person's unconscious. I think that is what happened in the example above. I believe, as did my esteemed colleague, that his client's low level of never-ceasing anxiety and depression was a result of his unconscious knowing. I do not proclaim to understand how this works. I only know what I have experienced and what others have shared with me about this phenomenon. I often wonder if this phenomenon is related to Albert Einstein's "spooky action at a distance" theory, or that of quantum entanglement—neither of which I fully understand, even though I have been studying for decades.

The following is another example of a protective secret gone awry:

A mother and father brought their sixteen-year-old daughter in with them for family therapy. They were concerned that she was violating curfew, and they believed she was having sex with her boyfriend. The mother, particularly, berated and scolded the daughter. I observed the mother becoming almost hysterical as she talked about what was going on with the daughter.

This was my clue that there was something more I needed to understand. I decided to meet with the parents for a session without the daughter present. When I met with the parents alone, I learned that the mother had gotten pregnant at sixteen and had given up that child for adoption. She had never shared this secret with her husband. I helped the two of them process this information. The husband was nonjudgmental and was able to be comforting and supportive to his wife.

I totally supported the wife/mother's right to privacy, but I also expressed some concern that *history can be repeated in a family*, especially when *shameful* information is not discussed and processed.

As I stated previously, what we often do not know consciously, we "know" at the unconscious level. This "knowing" can affect us at the emotional level. It can, and often is, expressed behaviorally, especially by children and teenagers.

The family returned with the daughter. The mother had shared and processed her secret with her husband, and now had decided to share her experience with her daughter. She did so in a calm manner with appropriate affect. The daughter went over to her mother, sat beside her, and wrapped her arms around her. The two of them cried together. The father reached out and touched them both lovingly.

The daughter said she understood her parents' concerns for her. She also said she did not think their concerns were necessary, but that she would comply with the set curfew.

The family had several more family sessions to work through the parent/teenager issues, particularly the concern about the daughter being sexually active. The tenor of the sessions changed dramatically as they truly attempted to listen and to understand one another.

I believe that this change was able to occur because the BIG secret, the mother getting pregnant and giving a child up for adoption, was out in the open.

The secrecy of adoption is not as prevalent as it once was. Early in my career, it was not uncommon for an individual who had been adopted to be unaware that this was the case. How the issue of adoption is addressed in the family has a tremendous impact on the family members. Adoption beliefs and stories impact assigned roles, relationship boundaries, and how individuals think about who they are in the world.

Protective secrets are often destructive secrets.

Destructive secrets are toxic and hold a certain amount of risk for at least one of the members of the family.

Some secrets are indeed *dangerous*. Certainly, secrets involving physical and sexual abuse are dangerous. Secrets regarding threats to self or others are dangerous. Secrets that involve breaking the law are dangerous.

For instance, a young man who had just started college came into therapy because a gang member with whom his older brother was involved had recently murdered this client's younger brother and sister in their home. His older brother was selling drugs out of their home. His uncle knew about this arrangement. The uncle, who had been a gang member himself, decided not to tell his sister, the client's mother.

Dangerous secret!

Secrets and Shame

Destructive secrets tend to promote the experience of *shame* for one or more of the family members involved. When one experiences shame, one may feel humiliated, embarrassed, unworthy, dishonorable, inadequate, and unable to feel safe enough to connect with others. Often when individuals experience shame, they believe that their whole being is flawed.

Feeling shame may be a result of something the individual did or believes they have failed at doing. In a family, the shame the individual members of the family feel is often about how they believe they are perceived by others outside the family because of their race, religion, sexual preference, or economic status. Or the individual members may experience shame because of the occurrence of something that has happened or is happening within the family that feels wrong or would be judged by the outside world as wrong. *It is shame that often fuels the keeping of secrets.*

I mentioned previously the concept of shared family secrets, secrets that the family shares but hides from the outside world.

Most often these secrets revolve around addiction, illegal actions, or physical and sexual abuse. Shared family secrets may not be carried by every member of the family, in that some members may not be aware of the secret. For example, in a family with a mother, father, daughter aged twelve, a son aged ten, and a daughter aged five, perhaps only the father, mother, and oldest daughter know that the mother's brother has molested the oldest daughter. The younger children may never be told. Of course, that does not mean that at some unconscious level they know that something terrible has happened to their sister. Unfortunately, it is often the victim that feels the shame. It is certainly not unusual for the victim to feel self-loathing and low self-esteem.

If a child is related to someone who is behaving shamefully, the child may feel ashamed. I have heard this so many times from adult children of alcoholics. After this many of years of practicing psychotherapy, I still feel sad when I am sitting with a person who as a child took on the shame of some adult who behaved shamefully. Children tend to believe they are responsible for or are "bad" because an adult in their lives abused, abandoned, or hurt them in some way. I see it as my job to help my client place the blame, shame, and *responsibility* where it belongs— on the perpetrator of the shameful behavior (usually an adult). I encourage my client to develop and practice self-compassion and self-nurturing, ultimately leading to self-forgiveness if that is indicated.

I feel so indebted to Oprah Winfrey. So many more women entered therapy to heal from abuse they had experienced once her show began in the mid-1980s. I believe she encouraged many, many women to talk about their experiences of abuse. She taught them that they could heal from the woundedness of abuse and gave them permission to seek help and to stop blaming themselves.

Shame Versus Guilt

Guilt and shame are often confused. When I was a young therapist, I remember a colleague saying, "Guilt is a useless emotion." I was sure he was wrong and have spent decades ruminating about his statement. I do think that when someone has done something wrong, it is appropriate for him to feel guilty. What I have observed, however, is that most of the time when an individual is feeling guilty, it is indeed not productive and is a waste of energy. Because guilt without *remorse* is useless. Feeling remorse and sadness pave the way for healing.

Example: A woman in her early sixties came to see me after she had been hospitalized for taking an overdose of pain pills. She said that she no longer wanted to live because of the guilt that she was feeling about not protecting her now-adult daughter from being sexually abused by her ex-husband, the daughter's father, when the daughter was younger.

She said that the guilt had been eating away at her for years, and she could not stand it any longer. I ask her if it was the guilt that she could no longer live with, or the shame she felt around the guilt. She described to me the difference. She said, "I feel guilty about what I *didn't* do, but it is the shame that is eating me alive." I explained to her that feeling guilty is feeling bad about an action taken or not taken. Feeling shame is about how we feel and judge ourselves, not just our actions. So not only do we think or say, "What I did was bad or wrong," but "I am bad or wrong."

Before coming to see me, she had tried to talk to her daughter, but her daughter did not want to be involved in an ongoing personal relationship. Guilt! Guilt! Shame! It consumed her.

So, my question to her was, "What do you wish you had done differently?" She gave me a number of answers that were often followed by a rationalization of why she had not chosen to do something different. For example, one of her answers was, "I thought about taking my daughter and running away, but I had nowhere to go." I have no doubt that at the time she believed this to be true. (Although I know of many mothers who did just that—left an abusive situation with nowhere to go.)

Little by little, I encouraged her to take responsibility for her decisions. As we journeyed along this course, I supported her acknowledging her remorse—the mental anguish of guilt connected to the sadness she felt for her daughter, for herself, for the situation. She soon realized that in her claiming her guilt to her daughter, saying "I was wrong. I am guilty. I did the best I could. I did not have any other options. I am sorry," her daughter heard only hollow words devoid of remorse and sadness. This was not enough for her daughter to reconnect with her. When my client moved from focusing only on her guilt to her feeling remorse and great sadness, she was aware that her internal emotional state had changed, thus allowing herself to have her sadness and grieve more fully. She was then able to talk with her daughter from a place of truth, remorse, and sadness, which opened the door for receptive communication. Her daughter became willing to have some limited contact with her. I encouraged them to get some family therapy to support them in the healing of their relationship. I am happy to say that this case had a "happy" ending.

In families in which family secrets carry *shame,* until the secrets and shame have been dealt with by the family members, then the embarrassment, humiliation, and shame may be passed on through generations. It is important that I reiterate some of the steps that can help with healing guilt and shame:

- It is essential to place the blame, shame, and *responsibility* where it belongs—on the person or persons who made the poor choice to commit shameful behavior.

- I encourage individuals to develop and practice self-compassion and self-nurturing, ultimately leading to self-forgiveness if that is indicated.
- If the individuals long to forgive those who did the wrongdoing, they absolutely need to forgive themselves first if they are holding any of the guilt and shame. Forgiving others and healing relationships can then follow if so desired.
- I believe it is worth repeating what I stated in the previous chapter: Forgiving does NOT mean forgetting. Forgiveness does not mean letting go of holding yourself or another accountable. The act of forgiving means releasing the emotional energy you have attached to a person or situation. Forgiving is a gift you give yourself.

Sweet Secrets and Necessary Secrets

There are toxic secrets and dangerous secrets. There are also necessary and "sweet" secrets.

Evan Imber-Black, director of Ackerman's Center for Families and Health and a faculty member at the Ackerman Institute for the Family, describes the idea of "sweet secrets" as being time-limited and for someone else's good. Examples are a gift, a surprise party—something another will enjoy.[2]

Then, there are necessary secrets. The women whom I have seen in therapy who suffer from domestic abuse have taught me about necessary secrets. Their "escape plan" obviously needs to be a secret that is kept from their abusers, because of the threat of perhaps even more violent abuse by the abuser.

I have had clients, friends, and family members who have been diagnosed with a severe or terminal illness and want to process this information themselves, and make plans, before sharing the information with others in their families.

As a therapist, it is not appropriate for me to tell clients what to do or not to do, but instead to help them identify the consequences of their choices.

Secrets and the individuals who hold them are each unique. There is no "one size fits all" when dealing with the issue of keeping or revealing a secret. If you are keeping a secret from family members, I suggest asking these questions:

- Whom does the secret protect? Self? Other?
- What is the worst thing that could happen if the secret is known?
- Could there be more harm than good if a secret is revealed?
- Is it possible that more harm is being done by not speaking the unspeakable?

If you are a secret bearer for someone else's secret or wrongdoing, ask yourself: Is doing so causing you stress and emotional pain? If so, are you willing to release this cumbersome role of carrying the secret and the guilt and shame that may accompany it?

REMEMBER: Family secrets can be a devastating force in a family system.

What we don't know CAN hurt us!

Reflections

Note to reader: I am not asking you to explore additional questions at the end of this chapter. I am suggesting that if you are carrying a secret that is "eating away at you" (yours or someone else's), consider getting help. Talk to a confidant, a religious advisor, or seek therapy.

If you have some internal "gut feeling" that there is something important in your family that you do not know, find the courage to ASK about it. Before doing so, however, get the support you need from family, friends, or a professional.

I encourage you to think about what your family's rules were about honoring a person's privacy and how that influences you in your current relationships.

Identify the ways you handle your need or desire for privacy. Be honest with yourself about the impact that this has on your relationships. If you believe that your "privacy needs" are hiding something that is relevant to another, you could be keeping a secret, rather than being private about something. Be sure you are practicing self-care when honoring your want or need for privacy. (Claiming privacy for illegal acts or to engage in something harmful to self or others is NOT self-care.)

That being stated, honoring your privacy wants and needs is essential to good mental health. It often requires you to set clear and firm boundaries between you and other members of your family.

Chapter Eight

How Powerful Are Stories, Myths, and Rituals?

The Shaping of Generations

We shall not cease from exploration
And the end of all our exploring
Will be to arrive where we started
And know the place for the first time.

T. S. ELIOT

Many stories or beliefs that we have about who we are have come from our families. These stories may be about us personally. Other family stories or myths are about the family as a whole. The stories and the myths may be based in reality, or may be the creation of one's imagination. Either way, these stories and myths define how the family and the individuals in the family see themselves in relationship to one another and the world. In this chapter I will illuminate the power of family stories and myths by sharing with you some examples from my life.

Myth #1: She Died Before I Was Born

As a young child, I grieved that I did not know my mother's mother. She died before I was born. Nonetheless, I have always felt that she was very important in my becoming who I am.

I was told that my grandmother died when she was fifty-four years old; my mother was twenty years old when her mother died.

My mother never talked much about her growing up, but it was always evident to me that she carried within her a deep sadness for losing her mother when she was a young woman. When I was around twelve, we traveled to Cleveland to see my mother's aunt and uncle who had known my grandmother when she was young. My great-uncle shared memories he had about my grandmother. He went on and on about how much I reminded him of my deceased grandmother. His statements impacted me in a way that was beyond my understanding.

In the home where I raised my three sons, I had above my bed some family photographs. One was a black and white photograph of my grandmother taken several years before her death; I have always loved this picture. My grandmother looks so beautiful with her white hair piled high upon her head and wearing a lovely white crocheted dress. The night of the day I turned fifty-three years old, I was sitting in bed reading. This photograph, which had been hanging on the wall above my bed for several decades, fell off the wall and landed face down in my lap. On the back of the photograph, my mother had written the date my grandmother was born and the date of her death. For some reason, I did the math. I did it again. I sat stunned. She had died at the age of fifty-two.

For much of my life, I had feared that I would die at the same young age that she had died. After all, my great-uncle had told me how much I reminded him of her! But that very day, I had my fifty-third birthday! I was so relieved! I felt peaceful and free now believing that I would have more time in this world.

The following day I was giving a workshop for women on transforming their lives. Here it was—in one brief moment, my life, my *belief*, transformed. I had created a myth about my own death based on the words of my great-uncle stating how very much I reminded him of my grandmother.

I have seen in my practice how often individuals carry a belief or fear that they will die at the same age as did a parent or grandparent. This may or may not be an irrational fear, but one I have learned many people believe consciously or carry deep within their psyches.

Myth #2: Real or Imagined

There have been many stories and myths in my family that have impacted me. When I was a teenager, I became very interested in the study of religion, which inspired me to learn more about my family's religious beliefs. I knew that my father's father came from an Irish Catholic family. I knew some of my father's cousins and knew that they were practicing Catholics. I asked my aunt why my grandfather had left the Catholic Church. She told me a story, which became part of the fabric of my life. It influenced my thoughts, beliefs, and biases.

When I was in my sixties, several years before the death of my aunt, I was visiting with her and recounted the story she had told me. I shared with her how I believed this story about my family's history had impacted me in my life. My aunt did not remember having ever told me this story, and she stated that the story I had believed most of my life was not entirely true. I remember feeling confused and angry. I remembered exactly where we were sitting when she told me the story. I knew that the myth had had great importance to me and was one that influenced my becoming a family therapist. My Aunt Helen—my father's younger sister, and his only sibling—loomed large in my life. She was a talented artist who brought fun, mystery, and excitement into my life. She also had a flair for the dramatic. She had told me this story when I was in my late teens. Now, let me clarify: This is the story I heard. Is it the story my aunt actually told me? Was it a dream?

Here is the story as I remember it being told:

My grandfather's family emigrated from Ireland before the Civil War, settling in southern Indiana along the Ohio River.

My great-grandfather, as a young man, became a medic during the Civil War. After the war, he continued practicing medicine in his community. The family was well-respected in their local community. Being good Irish Catholics, they attended mass regularly and had a prominent pew in the church.

As the story goes, after the death of my great-grandfather, my great-grandmother fell in love and got engaged to be married. The man to whom she was engaged was killed in a farming accident shortly before they were to wed. It soon became apparent that she was pregnant with his child. This created a scandal in the community. The family lost their standing in the church, and no longer had the prominent pew.

My aunt told me that one of my great-grandmother's sons, my grandfather's brother, became so distraught that he took his own life. And that this was why my grandfather was no longer a practicing Catholic and no longer believed in God.

As a young woman entering college, this story impacted me on so many levels. I was already keenly aware of there being so much injustice in the world. I was, after all, entering adulthood in the sixties. I loved studying sociology and psychology in school and found myself curious about issues of mental and emotional health. I was passionate about combating injustice, and hypocrisy remains disdainful to me.

When discussing this family story with my aunt shortly before her death, she told me that her father did not have a brother who took his own life. She said that other than that, she thought the story to be fairly accurate.

Discovering later in life that the story as I remembered it was inaccurate ultimately did nothing to dispel the power that it had on how I chose to think about religion and my worldview in general. So often, we live with myths that come out of our own interpretations and imaginations. What we hear may not always be what was spoken. What was spoken may or may not be fact, but becomes legend. Whether or not a myth is born out of reality or is created in one's mind, it carries with it tremendous influence on our lives.

These two stories of my family took on mythical meaning to me and greatly impacted my life. Family stories may be factual or contrived, yet they become myths, not because of their accuracy but because they become legendary.

Stories and myths handed down to us from our families can influence, and may even govern, how we think and feel about who we are and about how we view LIFE. They may be passed on between several generations or many generations. It is my belief that we humans long to have meaning. We have a deep desire to understand how we fit into the world. Family stories, myths, traditions, and rituals are so very important and alluring to us because they provide us with a backdrop from which we can move forward in our lives and in the world.

Having awareness and understanding of how our family's stories and myths have influenced us gives us the freedom to accept or refuse the beliefs we have about who we are and what we choose to do.

The Power of Legacy

In a previous chapter, I wrote about the concept of family legacy. A family's myths influence family legacy—those expectations and rules prescribed by one's family about how to be and how to live, think, and feel.

How we think and feel about our relationships and ourselves is based on the stories that we have been told or that we tell ourselves. If I tell myself I am not lovable, then I will recall the memories and the stories I have created around those memories that confirm my belief. If I tell myself that I cannot trust men or women or authority figures, then I will create and recall the stories that confirm that belief. Likewise, if I believe that I am a good person, I will recall the times that I can remember, which are now the stories that I tell myself, to back up this claim.

The stories and beliefs that we learn from our families instruct us on how to adapt to our environment. They have the power to contribute to our suffering or empower us to overcome or recover from the difficulties life presents to us.

I have chosen to practice psychotherapy in a nonprofit community-based counseling center. The philosophy of our center is to offer quality therapy to individuals, couples, and families no matter what they can afford to pay by offering a sliding fee.

In the fifty years that I have practiced at the center, many wonderful colleagues have come and gone. In the past decade, some have retired, but most of the ones who left went into private practice. I have thought about it often, as I knew it would be a more lucrative proposition. I have no doubt that one of the reasons I have been so loyal and committed to the nonprofit center is because of a larger-than-life myth that surrounds my family.

The Carney Grocery

I grew up in a small town in central Indiana where my father's parents owned a grocery store. I do not remember the grocery store, as it closed when I was a baby. The building that housed the grocery remained on the corner of the lot where my aunt and uncle lived. Their home had formerly been the home of my grandparents. The grocery store closed because my grandparents were getting older, and the next generation was not interested in running the grocery store. It was also the time when chain grocery stores were beginning to pop up in small towns across the country, making it much harder for the mom-and-pop grocery stores to exist.

The Carney Grocery has impacted all of my grandparents' six grandchildren, even though the oldest of us was not yet in elementary school when it closed. For me, it was the stories I heard from persons outside of my immediate family that became the most powerful. Several times, as a teenager, I would meet a person who had lived through the Great Depression or World War II and when I would introduce myself, I would see an expression of awe on their faces. They would ask me if I was related to Joe Carney. I would reply, "Yes. My father is Joe Carney, and my grandfather is Joe Carney." They would then ask if it was the Joe Carney who owned the Carney Grocery.

When I responded, "yes," they would begin to share their stories. I would hear how my grandparents gave them groceries during the Depression and WWII and that they were not able to pay my grandparents. They shared that my grandparents told them not to worry; that what they owed would be put on their bill and that they could pay when they could. These strangers told me how their families might have starved if it had not been for my grandparents' generosity. One person told me that my grandparents forgave their family's debt entirely. In order for my grandparents to pay their own debtors, they bartered property and valuables. I remember my grandmother sharing with me how grateful she was that they could help people in need during those sad and difficult times. Not only did my grandparents give to people in need of food, they also opened their home as a refuge for people who needed a place to stay. Some of those people could pay a little, while others could not.

This myth became the family motto: It is important to help those in need regardless of whether or not they can pay. So, it is no mystery why I have chosen to practice psychotherapy at a nonprofit counseling center all these many years.

Family stories and myths often convey the values that the family holds most dear. One of the values my father held most highly and spoke of frequently was that of *integrity*.

The story I recall when I think of my father and integrity is this: When my father was a young adult, he worked in the family grocery store. He got to know the suppliers well. At one point, one of the suppliers told him that a soft drink company was going to build a bottling plant in our town. He asked if my father would be interested in having that franchise. (Note: I am not sure it was considered a "franchise," or what term was used at that time in history.) If my father had taken that opportunity, we would have become quite wealthy.

My father refused this opportunity. He refused partly because he believed that this product was harmful to the human body. He said that he, in good conscience, could not produce and sell this product even though it meant declining the prospect of great financial rewards.

The bottling plant was built close to our house. We went by it daily. The family who owned the plant became quite wealthy. I remember at times thinking my father had made a "stupid" decision for not taking this opportunity when it was given to him. However, I came to understand that if my father had taken this opportunity, he would have had to forfeit his integrity. He would have gone against his own belief system. It was important to him that his actions and behaviors were in alignment with his values and beliefs. This story is about integrity. I took it to heart. Integrity remains one of the values I hold most dear.

I share these stories with you because I do believe they represent the power that our families' stories and myths play in our lives, be they factual or contrived.

Family Mottoes

Some family myths produce a family "motto." I am amused at how many mottoes influenced how my family lived.

"It is better to give than to receive."

"Integrity above all else."

"Only spend what you earn."

"An ounce of prevention is worth a pound of cure."

My mother's favorite: "Today is the tomorrow you worried about yesterday." This saying implied my mother's belief: worrying is a waste of time and energy. I am grateful to have learned that lesson so early in my life.

The list goes on and on. As I have explored the origins of the mottoes my family lived by, I have discovered that many of them were born out of the stories and myths that have been passed from generation to generation in my family.

As I observe today's young families, I feel concerned that there is a deficit in the sharing of family myths and stories. Everyone seems more interested in the stories that are being shared by little machines (iPads and cell phones) or giant television screens. Although, I must admit, I was impressed when my then six-year-old grandson thought he needed to teach me about Greek mythology and how it relates to the constellations. Something he learned from a machine.

I do implore you to turn off your machines and TALK to one another. Parents and grandparents, share your stories and myths. Yes, you will repeat yourselves. And, yes, your sharing may "bore" your offspring.

Do it anyway. Check back with them in twenty years.

Family Rituals and Traditions

Definition of *tradition*:

1. an inherited, established, or customary pattern of thought, action, or behavior
2. a belief or story or a body of beliefs or stories relating to the past that are commonly accepted as historical though not verifiable
3. the handing down of information, beliefs, and customs by word of mouth or by example from one generation to another without written instruction[1]

Rituals are embedded in traditions. Life-cycle transitions such as birth, graduation, marriage, and death are rich with ritual experiences. Participating in rituals helps to relieve the anxiety that is often experienced when change occurs. Every culture and religion has traditions and rituals built into them. Traditions offer stability and provide a sense of identity and belonging in a world that is constantly changing and periodically chaotic. Rituals are meaningful and powerful because they ignite something in us that goes beyond words and actions—often mysterious, even spiritual for some.

Of course, not all traditions and rituals hold great meaning for all of the participants. Some individuals experience such events as an obligation fraught with stress or foreboding.

There is a lot of overlap between something that is a tradition and something that is a ritual. Traditions usually have rituals that are essential to the experience. Traditions are generally passed down from generation to generation and practiced repeatedly. Even though rituals may be part of a tradition, they may also be experienced as a one-time event.

For example: I live by a river. When I moved in, there was a beautiful old oak tree whose large, heavy branches dipped down into the river. I named her Grandmother Tree. Sometimes at night when I could not sleep, I would sit in a comfy chair and stare out at her, silhouetted against the night sky. I felt a great connection with her. Her presence comforted me and inspired me.

One night, several years after I moved in, she fell into the river. She did so gracefully, so that none of the other trees or shrubs were damaged. The root ball stayed in the ground, so no harm was done to the river's edge. It was important to me to create a ritual to honor her years of giving, and of her transitioning to be in the river rather than on the bank where she had towered above many of the other trees.

I asked a friend who had studied native cultures to help me design a ritual. We burned sage. We each played our wooden flutes. We sang to the tree. We blessed the tree and her beautiful energy. Although I felt sad, I felt complete. Complete that I had honored her for her existence and for how very much she meant to me.

I encourage clients to design rituals to help them honor themselves, another person, an event, or a rite of passage. One of the important aspects of creating a ritual is that of honoring the past, the present, and the future. I also invite them to use as many of their senses as possible, as I believe this facilitates being in the fullness of the experience of the ritual rather than just "doing" the ritual.

One such ritual that has remained with me over the years involves a female client who had recently divorced. She had one child, a son who spent the first Christmas after her divorce with her. She so dreaded the Christmas that would follow, when her son would be with his father; the thought was devastating to her. I encouraged her to think of ways that she could take care of herself, and we explored numerous options. My client decided that rather than stay in bed and pull the covers over her head, she would create a one-time ritual. She was clear that she did not want to be with other family members or friends, knowing that she needed to be alone and create something unique and fitting for herself. She decided to go to a beach that was in reasonable driving distance. She packed some movies that she could watch on Christmas Day. She also took candles and scarves and other objects that she wanted available to create a ritual.

When we met before the holiday, I felt she was prepared and that she would get through Christmas, even though it would be with a heavy heart.

When I saw her for our appointment after the holidays, she exhibited contentment and peace. My client shared with me that she had created a beautiful ritual on the empty beach. Using her candles and her scarves, she created a dance. As she danced uninhibited on the beach, she breathed in the beach air, feeling Mother Earth against her feet. She heard and saw the ocean waves and felt the warmth from the sun on her face. She described the experience in a way that let me know that her ritual had helped her transition from being a married, full-time mom, to being a divorced, part-time mom. This was huge. Her ritual transition story inspires me still.

As meaningful and rich as rituals and traditions can be, there are situations when family traditions create stress. Traditions that create stress show up in many different ways. One that shows up in therapy frequently is when two people from different cultures with different family traditions form a couple (I maintain the belief that *every couple* is made up of two persons from different cultures). The couple is faced with decisions about how they are going to go forward as a newly formed family who remains connected to the families from which they came. The new couple must negotiate how they will participate with their respective families in old traditions and what new traditions they choose to establish.

The couple has to decide not only how to participate with their families but also how to engage with each other regarding the traditions and rituals they bring into the relationship. For instance, if one member of a couple grew up in a family that made a big deal of celebrating birthdays on the day of the actual birth, and they marry a partner whose family celebrated birthdays in a very low-key way and generally not on the birthday date, then it is quite possible that there will be some distress around rituals regarding birthdays.

This difference in how families of origin celebrate birthdays can lead to conflict or create distance in the couple's relationship. The person who is used to having her birthday celebrated on the actual date may feel hurt if her partner neglects to do so. The birthday individual may be able to rationalize and try to talk herself out of feeling disappointed, sad, or angry. She may label those feelings as childish. However, the feelings may continue to exist, nonetheless. When this kind of disappointment is experienced, it is common to want to shut down and distance or attack the other person. The birthday individual will likely express her disappointment in a way that will push the other away by pouting (distancing) or criticizing (attacking). Distance and distress occur either way. It takes compassion, understanding, and a willingness to cooperate and negotiate for the couple to decide how they are going to incorporate their family of origins' traditions and how to create their own.

Rituals and Traditions Around Loss

While there are cultural, religious, and familial traditions and rituals around grief that involve a death of a person, it is important to find ways to acknowledge other types of losses as well. Each life-cycle transition, even the ones that hold great promise, holds the potential for loss. One can be overjoyed with the promise that marriage holds, but with that gain one is giving up something. The "something" may be freedom, or it may be much less significant, like choosing to eat popcorn for supper. The number of single women in my world who eat popcorn for supper astounds me—but I have yet to have a couple share with me that they had popcorn for their supper. It is certainly possible that may be happening, I am just not aware.

Some other types of losses that I want to include are the loss of a beloved pet; the loss of a job, which may contribute to the sense of losing one's identity; the loss of an important relationship; the loss of youth (aging); and the loss of a dream. This list is certainly not exhaustive.

In our Western culture, we tend to minimize many of our losses. The loss of a dream is one such loss I experience many minimizing. We all have dreams of something we want for the future. A few such dreams may involve a love interest, giving birth to a child, creating something that is meaningful, or accomplishing a goal.

When I suggest to my clients that the depression they are experiencing may be related to some loss that they have not acknowledged or allowed themselves to grieve, they often seem confused and surprised. If the loss they are experiencing is a loss of a dream, they will often say to me, "How can I grieve something I never had?" A dream occupies one's internal space and utilizes one's energy. It is an emotional investment one makes for the future. For example, the individuals and couples who have been through extensive fertilization treatments that have not produced a child often experience tremendous loss and grief.

As previously stated, there are expected and unexpected normal life-cycle transitions, which often have rituals or traditions built around them to help facilitate these life shifts. There are also life-cycle transitions that are considered to be *idiosyncratic* life-cycle transitions. Imber-Black lists the following as examples of idiosyncratic life-cycle transitions:

> bicultural marriage, gay or lesbian marriage; families
> formed by adoption, especially when there is overt or
> covert nonsupport from family members; families formed
> by new birth technologies; the birth of a handicapped
> child; the birth or adoption of a child by an unmarried
> mother or father; pregnancy loss; forced separation
> through hospitalization, imprisonment, or terror;
> reunion after such separations; migration; . . . the end
> of non-married relationships; foster placement and the
> reunion after foster placement; sudden, unexpected or
> violent death, including suicide[2]

This list changes over time as it is shaped by broad social processes. It is not unusual for individuals to come to therapy to deal with stress, grief, anger, and confusion born out of the difficulties they have encountered because of an idiosyncratic life-cycle event.

Grief may be an individual journey or a communal process. In either case, it is important to allow the process to take its course. We don't get "over" grieving; we move through it. The amount of time it takes to move through grief is different for each individual. When there is a death of a loved one in a family, the individual members will express their grief differently and move through their grief on different time frames. These differences can foster tension and frustration among the family members. There are no rules for the "right way" to do this. The important thing is to be understanding and patient with self and others. Sharing rituals can be an important aspect of the healing process. *Process* is the key word here. It is not one and done!

I have had clients say to me, "I don't know how to grieve." To which I respond, "Of course you do. You are a human. We come into this world knowing how to grieve. You have to get out of your way and allow yourself to experience your grief."

If the ritual for grief comes out of a culture, religion, or family, it is most helpful to personalize it in some way to have meaning for you. If the ritual is one you are creating for yourself or with others, take time to sit with yourself and feel and think what you most want and need from the experience.

Give yourself time and space to grieve.

Remember that grieving can drain your energy and you may feel disoriented. This is normal. Be patient with yourself and others. It is also important that one not get stuck in grief. This may happen if we attempt to stifle our grief. We need to acknowledge and feel it in order to move through it.

When grieving, get support from others. Stay connected to people, pets, plants, and other living things. It can be useful to express your grief through art, music, and writing.

As a therapist, I have had the privilege of helping clients create and design meaningful rituals that support and facilitate the transitions that they are dealing with and for which they often do not have a clear, traditional method for doing so.

Rituals help us to transition, connect, and grow.

Create them. Treasure them.

They are sustenance for one's soul.

Meanings

Exploring your family's stories and myths and how they have impacted you can foster a deeper understanding and appreciation for how you became who you are. More important than the stories and myths themselves are the *meanings* that we give to them.

This is good news. We may or may not have the power to change a family myth or story, but we do have the power to decide what *meaning* we choose to give these myths and stories.

I am reminded of this quote by Maya Angelou, "You may not control all the events that happen to you, but you can decide not to be reduced by them."

A male client in his late fifties came to see me because he was experiencing a deep depression. As always, I took an extensive family history. When I take a family history, I often ask the clients about family myths or important stories they have been told about their families. This client told me about a family story that carried with it the message that life is one struggle after another with no relief between the struggles.

As he continued to talk about what was going on in his life, it became apparent that he was living his life in a state of anxiety because he was constantly waiting for the "other shoe to drop." This created in him a deep depression. As we explored this phenomenon, he became aware that there was no room in his life for joy. He was so focused on the potentially disastrous future that lay ahead that he was not in the present moment, where joy resides.

He had truly taken his family's story to heart. He had adopted the meaning that his family had given to the sad storytelling of struggles around immigration and untimely deaths in the family, stories that recounted supposed facts about the family's history. Sad, indeed.

As we worked together, he was able to let history be history. He decided that the meaning that his family had given to living life was theirs, not his. He decided to think of "life" as more than one struggle after another with no room for anything except hardship. The meaning he decided to give the story was that this story told of a sad and difficult time in the history of the family. He decided that it was not a prescription for the future.

Little by little, he permitted himself to be in the present. He learned to be aware when he was creating anxiety by living in the future and becoming more depressed by living in the past. I worked with him on how he could change his thinking and his behaviors to support his living in the present with less anxiety and depression. Since our stories are never finished, I encouraged him to continue *intentionally* writing his stories and creating meanings that comfort and inspire him.

Before we can free ourselves, we have to know from what we are freeing ourselves, and then claim ownership of our freed selves. As Toni Morrison stated in *Beloved*, "Freeing yourself was one thing, claiming ownership of that freed self was another."

Generating and evolving new stories or giving different meanings to existing stories gives us the power to free ourselves from scripts that no longer serve us.

Stories, Myths, and Rituals

1. Identify some of your family's stories and myths. How have they impacted you? Do you wish to change the meaning you or your family have given to these stories? If so, what would the new meaning be?

2. What "mottoes to live by" did you learn from your family? Which ones have you chosen to live by/not live by? Are there mottoes for living that you have adopted or would like to adopt?

3. What traditions and rituals were important to your family? Which ones remain important to you? Which ones do you no longer find meaningful?

4. Are there any new traditions you have established or wish to establish?

5. Acknowledge any new rituals you have designed or participated in that have contributed to your growth and healing.

6. Can you think of anything for which you would like to create a ritual?

May the Force be with you.

Epilogue

To paraphrase a question posed by my mentor, Richard E. Felder, "Isn't ALL therapy family therapy?"

My answer: YES!

No individual can be completely separate. We are biologically programmed to need connection from the very beginning of our existence. We are impacted by others and we impact others.

The purpose of therapy is to foster growth, change, and healing in our clients. Carl Rogers, the founder of Humanistic Psychology, worked from the belief that we humans have an innate capacity for growing and healing.[1] Humanistic Psychology and Family Systems Theory refuted the medical model of seeing patients as pathological or ill. Instead, these therapeutic models see clients as capable beings striving for wholeness who are helped or hindered by their relationships both past and present. In other words, Family Systems Theory views human suffering as a result of relational patterns and experiences as much as or more than being caused by pathology or deficits.

Hopefully this book has supported you in gaining awareness into how your family systems operate by presenting some of the basic family systems theoretical principles, and that this awareness and knowledge of your family will foster you claiming your power to be the person you desire to be, both relationally and intrapersonally. The ultimate goal is for individuals to have a greater understanding of their inner worlds through understanding their relationships with their families.

I encourage you to continue with your understanding of yourself and your family. I have included a list of resources at the end of this book that may interest you. Of course, I also recommend individual, couple, and family therapy with a therapist who works from a systems perspective.

One last query: I wonder how many of you who read this book came from a family who taught the usefulness of self-awareness? And if you did not, how do you think you came to value self-awareness?

Circling inward and outward through the labyrinth of our lives allows us to mindfully construct a more satisfying future.

WARNING: Do not get caught up in the past or in the future. Just visit. Your power for experiencing life to the fullest resides in the present.

When I was nineteen, I was trying to get to a location on the other side of the huge campus at Indiana University. A male on a motorcycle, whom I assumed was a fellow student, asked me if I wanted a lift. In those days, accepting such an offer from a stranger was not considered as dangerous as it is today. I gladly accepted and he took me to where I wanted to go. I got off the motorcycle and thanked the stranger. Without a word, he handed me a typewritten poem. I carried it with me for years and have often shared it with clients, particularly the last line.

Live Each Day to the Fullest

Live each day to the fullest.
Get the most from each hour, each day,
and each age of your life.

Then you can look forward with confidence,
and back without regrets.

Be yourself—but be your best self.
Dare to be different and to follow your own star.

And don't be afraid to be happy. Enjoy what is beautiful.
Love with all your heart and soul.

Believe that those you love, love you.

Forget what you have done for your friends,
and remember what they have done for you.

Disregard what the world owes you,
and concentrate on what you owe the world.

When you are faced with a decision,
make that decision as wisely as possible—then forget it.

The moment of absolute certainty never arrives.
S. H. PAYER

Note to Therapists:

The family therapy concepts I have presented in this book are equivalent to skimming the cream off the top of a gallon of fresh milk. What I have included in this book is a condensed version of the volumes of material written about the principles presented. Also, there are a number of concepts I did not include in this body of work. I encourage you to read more about those concepts you found most interesting.

If you have not studied Carl Rogers's work on Humanistic Psychology, I highly recommend doing so. I am not sure it is still being taught. I cannot imagine engaging as a therapist without his teachings being at the core of the work I do with my clients.

Acknowledgments

I want to thank everyone who has been a part of The Link Counseling Center from 1972 until the present. This includes the clients who have honored me with the privilege of working with them, students, supervisees, clinical colleagues, supervisors, and mentors, as well as administrative and volunteer staff. You have enriched my life beyond measure personally and professionally.

Thank you to Catherine McCall, a dear friend, a fellow family therapist, and author of *Never Tell*. When I decided to finish writing this book, I asked Cathy to read the first three chapters, which were written over a decade ago and were in rough, rough draft form. She was kind enough to tell me that they did not need to go into the round file (the wastebasket), and that she thought the idea had potential. Thus, I embarked on completing this book.

Thank you to Carol Powell and Cheryl Simon for lovingly offering to read the original manuscript, edit, and critique early on.

Thank you to the many family members and friends who have encouraged me and believed in me.

I am so appreciative of my literary agent, Emmanuelle Morgan of Stonesong Literary Agency, for so believing in my book and helping me to find a publisher who is dedicated to "getting this book into the world!"

Thank you to my editor, Haven Iverson of Sounds True, for her expert guidance, her enthusiasm, and her belief in the potential of my book to be a help to individuals and families.

Thank you to ALL of the Sounds True staff, who are so knowledgeable, relatable, skilled, and professional, for guiding me in the process of getting this book published.

Glossary

Acting out   Behavior that is considered problematic and is usually the manifestation of unconscious feelings or tensions producing internal stress and impulses.

Attachment Theory   A psychological model that attempts to describe the dynamics of long-term and short-term relationship dynamics between humans.

Autonomy   Freedom to have one's own thoughts, feelings, and actions.

Boundary   The abstract delineation between subsytems in the family, as well as between the family and the outside world.

Closed system   Resists interacting with others outside of the system. This resistance to change increases the likelihood for one or more of the individuals in the system to suffer mentally, emotionally, and relationally.

Detriangulation   Consciously withdrawing from a position of being aligned with one family member against another.

Differentiation of self   Separating one's intellectual and emotional functioning from one's family, thus being able to identify one's own thoughts and feelings and make choices honoring one's self.

Dyad   A temporary or long-term relationship between two people.

Dysfunction   An impaired ability to cope, particularly under stress.

Emotional cutoff   Denying the importance of any unresolved emotional ties to one's family by emotionally withdrawing or running away.

Enmeshment   A family system with diffuse boundaries between the members where individuals are overly involved in one another's lives, rendering individuation and autonomy difficult.

Extended family   Those family members that are beyond the immediate nuclear family of parents and their children, such as grandparents, aunts, uncles, and cousins.

Family life cycle   The stages of development that the family system experiences as it processes through the developmental stages of the individual members.

Family of origin   The family into which one is born or adopted.

Family Systems Theory   A psychological theory that identifies the family as an emotional unit of interlocking relationships understood from a historical and transgenerational perspective, which focuses on relationship dynamics and how the family organizes itself regarding hierarchy and functioning.

Fusion   The merging of intellectual and emotional functioning of individual family members with one another.

Genogram   A pictorial display of a family's relationship system, including the reoccurring transgenerational patterns of behavior and hereditary tendencies in at least three generations.

Identified patient   The individual in the family with the presenting problem for which therapy is being sought.

Intrapsychic   What is happening within the mind or the psyche of an individual, particularly when the individual is dealing internally with conflicting forces.

Nuclear family   A family composed of one or two parents and their offspring, living together or functioning as a family unit.

Open system   A system with flexible, permeable boundaries that allows for interaction between the individuals in the family as well as the subsystems within the family, and is amenable to the family relating to the world outside of the family system.

Power   Having influence, authority, and control over an outcome.

Reframing   Describing perceived problematic behavior in a more positive perspective, thus giving the behavior new meaning.

Rituals   Activities designed to mark significant occasions or transitions in life.

Scapegoat   The family member, often the identified patient, who is blamed for the wrongdoings, mistakes, or faults of others.

Sibling position   The birth order of children in a family, which has an impact on their personalities and how they relate to themselves as well as others in the present and the future.

Structure   The organization of the family regarding boundaries and hierarchy.

Subsystem   A grouping within a larger system that has its own specified functions and roles.

System   An organization of interacting units or component parts.

Transgenerational pattern   A pattern or process occurring over several generations, such as the passing from one generation to the next of beliefs, behaviors, patterns of interaction, or prescribed family roles and function.

Triad   A three-person relationship.

Triangle   A three-person system that is created when a two-person emotional system is under stress and recruits a third person to stabilize the dyad.

Triangulation   Occurs when there is stress in a relationship between two people and a third person is recruited to reduce anxiety and gain stability.

Notes

Chapter 2: Who's in Charge?

1. Monica McGoldrick and Randy Gerson, *Genograms in Family Assessment* (New York: W. W. Norton, 1985).
2. Salvador Minuchin, *Families and Family Therapy* (Cambridge, MA: Harvard University Press, 1974).

Chapter 3: Is It Safe to Say What You Mean and to Mean What You Say?

1. Paul Watzlawick, Janet Beavin Bavelas, and Don D. Jackson, *Pragmatics of Human Communication: A Study of Interactional Patterns, Pathologies, and Paradoxes* (New York: W.W. Norton, 1967).
2. Virginia Satir, *The New Peoplemaking* (Palo Alto, CA: Science and Behavior Books, 1972), 30.
3. Satir, *The New Peoplemaking*.

Chapter 4: How Much Togetherness?

1. John Byng-Hall, "Evolving Ideas about Narrative: Re-editing the Re-editing of Family Mythology," *Journal of Family Therapy* 20, no. 2 (May 1998): 133–142, doi.org/10.1111/1467-6427.00074.
2. John Bowlby, *Attachment and Loss, Vol.1: Attachment*, 2nd ed. (New York: Basic Books, 1969).

3. Daniel J. Siegel, *The Developing Mind: Toward a Neurobiology of Interpersonal Experience* (New York: Guilford, 2012).

4. Murray Bowen, *Family Therapy in Clinical Practice* (New York: Jason Aronson, 1978).

5. This quote, commonly attributed to Viktor Frankl, is one I have heard and read many times over, but it does not seem to be verifiable in this exact format. Certainly, Frankl's writings hold the "meaning" of this quote. Since it is one of my favorites, I wanted to share it with you.

6. Robert Waldinger, "What Makes a Good Life? Lessons from the Longest Study on Happiness," January 25, 2016, TED video, 12:46, youtube.com/watch?v=8KkKuTCFvzI.

Chapter 5: Why a Three-Legged Stool?

1. Murray Bowen, "The Use of Family Theory in Clinical Practice," in *Changing Families: A Family Therapy Reader,* ed. Jay Haley (New York: Grune and Stratton, 1971), 163–71.

2. Daniel J. Siegel, *The Developing Mind: Toward a Neurobiology of Interpersonal Experience* (New York: Guilford, 1999).

3. Heinz Ansbacher and Rowena Ansbacher, eds., *The Individual Psychology of Alfred Adler: A Systematic Presentation in Selections from His Writings* (New York: Harper Perennial, 1964).

Chapter 6: Who Owes What to Whom?

1. Ivan Boszormenyi-Nagy and Geraldine M. Spark, *Invisible Loyalties: Reciprocity in Intergenerational Family Therapy* (Maryland: Harper & Row, 1973).

2. Kenneth S. Kendler, Christopher G. Davis, and Ronald C. Kessler, "The Familial Aggregation of Common Psychiatric and Substance use Disorders in the National Comorbidity Survey: A Family History Study," *British Journal of Psychiatry* 170, no. 6 (June 1997): 541–48, doi.org/10.1192/bjp.170.6.541.

3. Elizabeth Kübler-Ross, *On Death and Dying* (New York: Macmillan, 1969).

4. Philip J. Guerin et al., *The Evaluation and Treatment of Marital Conflict: A Four-Stage Approach* (New York: Basic Books, 1987).

Chapter 7: Keep or Reveal a Family Secret?

1. Naima Brown-Smith, "Family Secrets," *Journal of Family Issues* 19, no.1 (1998): 20–42, doi.org/10.1177 /019251398019001003.

2. Evan Imber-Black, "Creating Meaningful Rituals for New Life Cycle Transitions," in *The Expanded Family Life Cycle: Individual, Family, and Social Perspectives*, 3rd ed., ed. Betty Carter and Monica McGoldrick (Boston: Allyn and Bacon, 1999), 204.

Chapter 8: How Powerful Are Stories, Myths, and Rituals?

1. *Merriam-Webster.com Dictionary*, s.v. "tradition," accessed March 21, 2022, merriam-webster.com/dictionary/tradition.
2. Evan Imber-Black, "Creating Meaningful Rituals for New Life Cycle Transitions," in *The Expanded Family Life Cycle: Individual, Family, and Social Perspectives*, 3rd ed., ed. Betty Carter and Monica McGoldrick (Boston: Allyn and Bacon, 1999).

Epilogue

1. Carl R. Rogers, *On Becoming a Person: A Therapist's View of Psychotherapy* (Boston: Houghton Mifflin, 1995).

Resources

Resources for All

Bolton, Iris, and Mitchell, Curtis. *My Son . . . My Son . . . A Guide to Healing After Death, Loss, or Suicide*. Atlanta: Bolton Press, 2017.

Iris, with the assistance of her father, Curtis Mitchell, describes in detail the journey she made after the devastation of losing her son by suicide and the step-by-step healing that took place in her life. In Iris's second book, *Voices of Healing and Hope: Conversations on Grief after Suicide*, she identifies eight issues that are among the most difficult for survivors based on an informal survey of family members impacted by suicide.

Brown, Brené. *The Gifts of Imperfect Parenting: Raising Children with Courage, Compassion, and Connection*. Original audio. CO: Sounds True, 2013.

This lovely audio program encourages parents to embrace their imperfections, thus helping them to teach their children to have the courage to be authentic, develop compassion toward themselves and others, and inspire the sense of connection that gives true purpose and meaning to life.

Frankl, Viktor. *Man's Search for Meaning*. Boston: Beacon Press, 2006.

Frankl wrote this book in 1946 out of his experience in a concentration camp in Germany. Frankl concludes that the meaning of life is found in every moment of living; life never ceases to have meaning, even in suffering and death.

Gottlieb, Lori. *Maybe You Should Talk to Someone: A Therapist, Her Therapist, and Our Lives Revealed*. New York: Houghton Mifflin Harcourt, 2019.

A fun read that takes the reader into the world of psychotherapy from both the perspective of the therapist and the patient. Delightful and informative.

Hollis, James. *What Matters Most: Living a More Considered Life.* New York: Gotham Books, 2009.

Hollis guides readers in discovering what it means to truly live life to its fullest, most meaningful state, and to fully engage as citizens of the world.

Johnson, Sue. *Hold Me Tight: Your Guide to the Most Successful Approach to Building Loving Relationships.* United Kingdom: Little, Brown, 2011.

This book makes the principles of attachment theory available to the readers and instructs them on how to create and improve their relationships.

Lerner, Harriet. *Harriet Lerner on Mothers and Daughters: Breaking the Patterns That Keep You Stuck.* Original audio. CO: Sounds True, 2009.

Dr. Lerner helps us to better understand the mystery of the mother-daughter bond and guides us in how to stay connected (and stay ourselves) when differences arise. She offers specific skills and guidelines for changing the patterns that keep us stuck.

Marchiano, Lisa. *Motherhood: Facing and Finding Yourself.* CO: Sounds True, 2021.

Lisa draws from her in-depth knowledge of Jungian psychology and symbolic research, sharing insights into timeless archetypes by using the ancient tradition of storytelling to truly empower the experience of motherhood. She invites the reader on an inner journey to clarify their values and to embrace parts of themselves they have forgotten or disowned.

McCall, Catherine. *Never Tell: A True Story of Overcoming a Terrifying Childhood*. Scotts Valley, CA: CreateSpace, 2014.

This book is a must read for anyone who has suffered childhood sexual abuse, loves someone who did, or works with survivors.

Papernow, Patricia. *Surviving and Thriving in Stepfamily Relationships: What Works and What Doesn't*. New York: Routledge, 2013.

Papernow draws on current research, a wide variety of clinical modalities, and thirty years of clinical work with stepfamily members to describe the special challenges stepfamilies face.

Pittman, Frank. *Private Lies: Infidelity and the Betrayal of Intimacy*. New York: W. W. Norton, 1990.

Dr. Pittman identifies four basic patterns of infidelity: the accidental encounter, habitual philandering, marital arrangements, and romance; and discusses how to limit the damage that affairs do, as well as offering practical suggestions on how to make a marriage work.

Tatkin, Stan. *We Do: Saying Yes to a Relationship of Depth, True Connection, and Enduring Love*. CO: Sounds True, 2018.

Stan espouses relationship success if partners take care of each other in a way that ensures both "feel safe, protected, accepted, and secure at all times." This book is a great guide for helping couples determine if they are "right for each other" and how to be a "we."

Resources for Therapists

Bowlby, John. *Attachment and Loss, Vol. 2: Separation—Anxiety and Anger.* New York: Basic Books, 1979.

    A classic.

Gottman, Julie S. and Gottman, John M. *10 Principles for Doing Effective Couples Therapy.* New York: W.W. Norton, 2015.

    A great book describing the basic steps of working with couples.

Joseph, Stephen. *Positive Therapy: Building Bridges Between Positive Psychology and Person-Centered Psychotherapy.* London: Routledge, 2015.

    Joseph is masterful at explaining the importance of Carl Rogers's work.

Napier, Augustus Y. and Whitaker, Carl A. *The Family Crucible: The Intense Experience of Family Therapy.* New York: Harper and Row, 1978.

    A wonderful introduction to family therapy in which the Brice family's experience alternates with commentary on the process and its implications for patients and therapists.

Porges, Stephen W. *The Pocket Guide to the Polyvagal Theory.* New York: W.W. Norton, 2017.

    Porges's work in the field of neurophysiological theory is enlightening and of great clinical importance. This book is a guide to understanding the human nervous system.

Rogers, Carl R. *Client-Centered Therapy: Its Current Practice, Implications, and Theory.* United Kingdom: Little, Brown, 2021.

    Invaluable.

Schwartz, Richard. *No Bad Parts: Healing Trauma and Restoring Wholeness with the Internal Family Systems Model.* CO: Sounds True, 2021.

    Understanding Dr. Schwartz's brilliant theoretical model of Internal Family Systems has been invaluable to me and my work for decades. If you are a therapist, I hope you will take the time to learn more about this model. We all have many "parts." Helping our clients to understand and befriend their parts is such an amazing healing process.

Siegel, Daniel J. *The Mindful Therapist: A Clinician's Guide to Mindsight and Neural Integration*. New York: W. W. Norton, 2010.

A beautiful book on the usefulness of mindfulness in creating the healing relationship between the client and the therapist.

Yalom, Irvin. *Love's Executioner: And Other Tales of Psychotherapy*. New York: Basic Books, 2012.

In his classic, bestselling work, the masterful therapist and novelist Irvin Yalom describes his sometimes tragic, sometimes inspiring, and always absorbing encounters with patients.

When I began my journey to becoming a family therapist, there were no programs in universities offering courses in Marriage and Family Therapy as a discipline. We early practitioners learned by attending workshops and training programs, as well as reading books by the masters. I am grateful for this experience and have chosen to share some of these classic books with you that are not included in the endnotes.

Bowen, Murray. *Family Therapy in Clinical Practice*. New York: Jason Aronson, 1978.

Haley, Jay. *Uncommon Therapy: The Psychiatric Techniques of Milton H. Erickson, MD*. New York: W.W. Norton, 1973.

Hoffman, Lynn. *Foundations of Family Therapy: A Conceptual Framework for Systemic Change*. New York: Basic Books, 1981.

Madanes, Cloé. *Strategic Family Therapy*. San Francisco, CA: Jossey-Bass, 1981.

Watzlawick, Paul, Weakland, John, and Fisch, Richard. *Change: Principles of Problem Formation and Problem Resolution*. New York: W.W. Norton, 1974.

The following book is not a Family Therapy classic. I include it because Richard Felder was my beloved mentor and supervisor. He, along with Carl Whitaker, Thomas Malone, and others, established the Atlanta Psychiatric Clinic and were pioneers in Experiential Psychotherapy.

Felder, Richard E. and Weiss, Avrum G. *Experiential Psychotherapy: A Symphony of Selves.* Maryland: University Press of America, 1991.

A beautiful read that explores the self-of-the-therapist and the creativity of Experiential Psychotherapy.

About the Author

Elaine Carney Gibson has been a practicing psychotherapist for fifty years in Atlanta, Georgia. She sees individuals, couples, and families, specializing in relationship therapy. She taught graduate courses in Marriage and Family Therapy for many years. Elaine is a Licensed Professional Counselor and a Licensed Marriage and Family Therapist in the state of Georgia. She is a Certified Professional Counselor Supervisor and is an Approved Supervisor and a Clinical Fellow of the American Association for Marriage and Family Therapists. She is the Director of the Marriage and Family Therapy Training Institute of The Link Counseling Center in Atlanta, Georgia.

Elaine remembers that even when she was in elementary school, she would think about how family systems operate and how the stories told in the family shaped the individuals in the family system. She discovered Family Systems Theory shortly before having her first child. Elaine considers raising her three sons as one of her greatest learning experiences.

She believes that what has kept her thriving as a psychotherapist is the fact that she remains excited about her work and unwaveringly believes that there is always more to learn.

You can learn more by visiting elainecarneygibson.com.

About Sounds True

Sounds True is a multimedia publisher whose mission is to inspire and support personal transformation and spiritual awakening. Founded in 1985 and located in Boulder, Colorado, we work with many of the leading spiritual teachers, thinkers, healers, and visionary artists of our time. We strive with every title to preserve the essential "living wisdom" of the author or artist. It is our goal to create products that not only provide information to a reader or listener but also embody the quality of a wisdom transmission.

For those seeking genuine transformation, Sounds True is your trusted partner. At SoundsTrue.com you will find a wealth of free resources to support your journey, including exclusive weekly audio interviews, free downloads, interactive learning tools, and other special savings on all our titles.

To learn more, please visit SoundsTrue.com/freegifts or call us toll-free at 800.333.9185.

sounds true
WAKING UP THE WORLD